THE
INNER GLIDE

THE INNER GLIDE

The Tao of Skiing,
Snowboarding, and Skwalling

Patrick Thias Balmain

Translated by Jon E. Graham

Destiny Books
Rochester, Vermont

Destiny Books
One Park Street
Rochester, Vermont 05767
www.DestinyBooks.com

Destiny Books is a division of Inner Traditions International

Originally published in French under the title *La glisse intérieure* by Le Souffle d'Or, BP
3 – 05300 Barret-sur-Méouge, France, www.souffledor.fr
First U.S. edition published in 2007 by Destiny Books

Library of Congress Cataloging-in-Publication Data
Balmain, Patrick Thias.
  [Glisse intérieure. English]
  The inner glide : the Tao of skiing, snowboarding, and skwalling / Patrick Thias
Balmain ; translated by Jon E. Graham.
    p. cm.
  Summary: "Skiing can be a path to higher spiritual awareness, contributing to
centering, ego effacement, and the search for perfect mental stillness"—Provided by
publisher.
  Includes bibliographical references and index.
  Translation of: La glisse intérieure.
  ISBN-13: 978-1-59477-160-6 (pbk.)
  ISBN-10: 1-59477-160-X (pbk.)
  1. Skis and skiing. 2. Snowboarding. 3. Meditation. I. Title.
  GV854.B33613 2007
  796.93—dc22

                                                                    2007015029

Printed and bound in the United States by P. A. Hutchinson

10   9   8   7   6   5   4   3   2   1

Text design by Virginia Scott Bowman
This book was typeset in Sabon with Gentle Sans and Avenir as display typefaces

Images used under liscence from Shutterstock, Inc.: page vi photo © by Martin
Trajkovski; page viii photo © by Maxim Petrichuk; page 44 photo © by Ilja Mašik;
page 69 photo © by Mark Yuill; page 82 photo © by Taylor Jackson; page 116
photo © by Galina Barskaya; page 142 photo © by Juha Tuomi; background snow
texture photo © by avatavat.

Contents

Acknowledgments

My thanks to Anne-Laure Guillot, Laurence Corby, and Yves Balmain who helped me complete this book.

To my students, who participated (albeit unaware) in my personal development and my own evolution thanks to or because of their conduct on the snow.

To the photographers Mario Colonel, Serge Strippentoir, and Skis Lacroix, who generously provided photos for this book.

To the authors cited in the bibliography.

To the mountain and to the snow, which we need to protect.

Introduction

When the snowboard first made its way to France, there were only a handful of us who used it, and no standard techniques had yet been worked out. We discovered this new skiing method on our own and used the most rudimentary equipment, often manufactured in a garage. Skiers "splintered" into isolated groups, and every instructor conducted his personal research in his own little niche.

In 1985, I opened one of the first snowboard schools in France, in Valfréjus. To satisfy my students' hunger for new sensations and techniques, I was forced to construct a snowboarding instruction method.

As I tried to put the technical progression of the snowboarder down on paper, I quickly realized that I had a tendency to merely repeat the models and mechanisms I had picked up from my training as a ski instructor. Yet, in reality, that is not what I was truly teaching at all, on skis or on snowboards.

My teaching method primarily consisted of solutions and recipes that simply responded to the stances of my students on the slopes. I would not say that my teaching method was well structured; rather, it was charged with feeling. I had acquired experience. I had drifted away from traditional teaching methods, but without having formulated a new method. I managed to guide my students to greater efficacy, but when it came to organizing and presenting those teachings in writing, I was completely blocked.

The main problem, it seemed to me, was that I found contact with my students to be an enormous drain on my energy. Their dilemmas became mine. I became one with their blocks, with no distance or detachment.

Though I didn't grasp it immediately, the real work I was engaged in at that time was, first and foremost, a quest motivated by a desire for personal development.

A number of questions presented themselves in quick succession. It is said that the question holds the answer. Not always! For instance, I had briefly tied myself in knots trying to answer the question: "Why does a board turn?" Discovering the causes of phenomena is no easy task—that question led me to start investigating the why of everything. But I still found it impossible to grasp any clear answer. My question had been poorly posed. My understanding and analysis were partial and incomplete, like a jigsaw puzzle of a great tree from which pieces were missing. I had one piece of the root here, another one there, several pieces of the trunk over here, and a couple pieces of the branches over there. I was still missing a large number of the pieces I needed for the tree to express its verticality, its balance, its strength, and its harmony.

Starting from this observation, my quest was long and sometimes painful. Someone who thought he knew everything had become a beginner again. Everything had to be broken apart, and I had to completely empty myself of all my knowledge and all my certainties. I began an unlearning process. Without an instructor to show the way, without a flesh and blood teacher, the path I had embarked upon became arduous.

At this time I could not even begin to imagine the impact that taking these steps would have on my life. To make a clean slate of my experience as a skier, and thereby of my education, caused an incredible upheaval. Over the course of time I had—with the help of my entourage—constructed a shell, and here I was taking it off one layer at a time. Once I reached a point where practically nothing remained of that shell, the emptiness it created within me created a terrible anxiety. Not only did it give me the sensation that death was knocking at my door, but that it was knocking at a door that no longer existed. In hindsight, I realize my feeling was not so disproportionate: I was really dying. I was not perishing physically but I was dying to myself, my former self.

A tornado was spinning through my mind. I began to feel the nature of the world's equilibrium and at the same time it filled me with terror. The sensations of paradise-like balance that filled me at times terrified me, because, being a good Westerner as I am, I unconsciously believed that paradise was not in this world, and I wanted to live. I wanted to stop everything I was going through and recover the stability I had lost. But it was too late for that; I had cut the moorings of my certitudes and was sailing on the raging sea of my discoveries, and the emotions of uprootedness that accompanied them. My only remaining point of attachment was my body. I anchored myself to it securely. This state of things would go on for days, weeks, even months.

One day I was bringing some hikers to make a climb in Vanoise National Park. While watching and listening to one of my clients I saw myself as if in a mirror. We did not resemble each other physically, but in our approach to life we were twins. Like me, he wanted to grasp everything, understand everything, and absorb everything—he wanted, in a way, to find the Holy Grail. That day I could see all my own pretensions and greed in the way he looked at the world. I had been trying to grab something that was impossible to grasp. I had understood nothing.

I began reading books and following practices from a wide variety of philosophies: yoga, Zen, the martial arts, tai chi chuan, qi gong, physics, astronomy, the Alexander Technique, personal development. I transformed from someone who was a doer and told others how to do into someone who listened.

The higher the piles of books I was reading and the heaps of notes I was writing grew, the greater the clarity I felt in my mind. Reconciling myself to who I was at that time, I gradually emptied myself. I began to comprehend this will to psychologically possess what was outside of me.

This journey carried me into my deepest inner self. My physical being became a three-stage vehicle: my body, my heart, my head. Little by little I learned to recognize how each of them functioned, how to pacify them and put them in tune with each other. I steeped myself in the teachings coming from other disciplines and other cultures, but skiing remained my chief support, my experimentation center. I abandoned the idea of seizing the meaning, the *why* of the world, to experience things internally and in awareness. It was a rebirth.

Gradually the questions became more specific—and more essential as well. The initial question transformed from "Why does a board turn?" into "How does a board turn?" The difference may appear nuanced and subtle, but it was this question that pulled me into a journey both internal and external.

With the question made clear, the answer became more tangible. Like a painter who can compose with an infinite of subtle hues and bring them to "life" on the canvas from a simple palette of colors, the skier who understands the actual physical principles of gliding over snow can, by carrying out well thought out choices and combinations, move with grace and harmony.

I gradually drew further and further from the standard technical handbook, which is a repertoire of codified gestures, toward an approach based on the study of physical phenomena and their conscious utilization. This was a major step. I set myself the task of making a list of the physical gestures distinctive of gliding and their implication for the skier and snowboarder. The study of these phenomena, with the snowboard as the chief reference, opened my eyes about the technique of skiing. A connection was forged between the different disciplines. The backdrop for each of them was gliding, a purely physical phenomenon, that the "artist" used more or less consciously. Whether we have one board or two beneath our feet, we are subject to the same physical laws.

It was in this realization that my interest in biomechanics emerged as the logical next step. Respect for the physical laws involves respecting the body and the alignment of its joints. My knees, which were quite fragile as a result of car accidents and accidents on the slopes, acted as excellent indicators of pressure and twisting.

In 1989, I spent a lot of my time alpine snowboarding. The position of the lower body and the feet facing sideways and the upper body facing forward, which the technique of that time required, created a great deal of pain in my back and knees. My thoughts on how to solve this problem then led me to create a new kind of equipment that would be more respectful to the body and bring unrivaled performance and savings in energy. I called this equipment a skwal.

Three years passed between my first cobbled-together invention and the prototype model. I shared my new pleasure with numerous skiers and snowboarders and, to meet the rising demand caused by their infatuation, I started manufacturing boards, initially with the support of Lacroix Skis and then under my own brand name, Thias Skwal. I cannot say that the worlds of industry and finance welcomed me with open arms.

The seasonal aspect of the activity, the phenomenon of the fast-growing snowboard craze, and the chilly attitude of the ski manufacturers did not facilitate the raising of funds necessary to launch the skwal. As is the case with any new invention, there is a time for observing and a time for adopting. If you are able to find good means to communicate and promote your product to help launch it, it will become viable much sooner as a business activity. The skwal needed a great deal of capital to ensure this: a successful launch of the skwal required manufacturing, marketing, promotion, and communication. Like most of the small snowboard manufacturers, I was obliged to stop operating my business. Fortunately, Lacroix continues to produce skwals today and other new manufacturers continue to appear in countries outside France. As for me, I have gone back to my first loves: the mountain and skiing.

During this same time I continued my exploration of other fields of activity. Physical laws are not the cause of everything. The skier or snowboarder does not function like a machine. He is subject to doubts, hopes, fears, beliefs, and so forth that shape his behavior. Understanding human psychology is no easy task. I had to turn to approaches that were new to my experience. It was necessary for me to observe and understand the psychological and emotional mechanisms in which I was evolving. In this regard, the martial arts approach was of great aid to me, not for its martial aspects but rather for the way it teaches a person to be fully present in the moment and situation. Eastern psychology allowed me to better grasp the relationship between human and environment. The quest for new sensations by means of skiing and other gliding sports was gradually transformed into listening to nature and embarking on a journey within. Instead of trying to create a simple technical and practical manual, I was now focusing my attention on an overall study of the skier—above all, myself—on three different planes: psychological, emotional, and physical.

Two years ago a woman friend who I had not seen for more than twenty years paid me a visit in Courchevel. She had left France to live in China, and I had received no further signs of life from her in the ensuing years. When she arrived for this surprise visit, the snow had been falling continuously, but even so the weather conditions were fine for a ski. I had a very clear memory of her skiing level from years previous. I remembered that she skied well, although with what we call a "Parisian" style. This means she skied in a floating and distinguished manner, keeping the skis together and holding the body erect while weaving from right to left, a technique that allowed her to descend most trails. But on that day I wondered how she would make out in this fresh snow after twenty years without skiing.

To my great surprise, not only did my friend ski well on the trails, but she was good off the trails as well. The deep snow that flew over our shoulders at every turn did not scare her in the least. She no longer skied the way she had before leaving for China. Her placement was impeccable. Her low stance guaranteed good stability, and she could string together curves on the steep slopes off the trails. It astonished me to see her ski this way! In my opinion, it was impossible to make this kind of progress without skiing. She was hiding something from me. I questioned her about what she had been doing during the last twenty years, what kind of sports activities she had been practicing. She told me that during her years in China, she had been practicing tai chi chuan with a teacher who lived in the mountains. She did not have the impression that she was now a better skier. She made sure to mention the two falls she took at the beginning of our afternoon, caused by the drifts of freshly fallen snow, which in her opinion was proof of her low level of expertise. For me, it demonstrated a lack of experience with powder, but it also showed that she possessed a great sense of balance, which in this instance was learned elsewhere than on snow.

Here, right before my eyes, was proof of the well-founded nature of the steps I had been taking. I was already convinced of it from my personal experimentation, but here she confirmed it and spurred me on to carry my work through to the end. Until this experience I had felt isolated and out of step in the ski environment. I guess I needed validation and recognition at this moment, and she seemingly appeared out of nowhere to bring me the proof for which I was unconsciously looking in the way she could move on the slopes.

When we ski (or practice any other gliding sport) everything immediately takes on greater proportions, and this is the reason it gives us pleasure: we feel that we are truly alive! The slightest gesture will have repercussions on our balance. With speed, obstacles loom up suddenly. Emotion surges up. The body becomes taut. The mind accelerates.

In the practice of tai chi chuan, the movements are slow, and internal shifts are subtle and difficult for the novice to perceive. To become masterful at the practice requires a long apprenticeship period that can appear austere. It is the exact opposite in skiing. Everything is disproportionate and strong. Sensations, emotions, tensions—in the beginning, everything in skiing is too intense, whereas in tai chi chuan everything is too calm. These two activities are perceived to be different from each other, even opposites, but in truth, at the end of the path the purpose is the same: harmony, balance, and taking joy in movement.

This period of study was quite beneficial to me and I was able to grasp the sense of nonduality inside of me, the sense of a middle and balanced way between extremes. One summer day when I was strolling through the tiny streets of Bonneval-sur-Arc, a typical small village of the Haute Maurienne area, I saw a father taking a picture of his three children sitting on the steps of a barn. Like on the temples of Angor Wat, I saw the three faces in one, as an expression of nonduality. With a broad smile on his face, the first was expressing his joy at being photographed; the second, visibly upset at having to stop what he was doing to sit still for a photo, was frowning; and the third, in the middle, was serenely radiant, like the Mona Lisa or Buddha. He was halfway between the two states of being his brothers were expressing. This touched me quite deeply. How was it possible for a simple moment like this to sum up so perfectly everything I had been reading and experiencing? The children in this scene were not aware of what kind of picture they were offering me. This representation awoke within me an awareness of the dynamic equilibrium between the opposites. I discovered later on that this aspect in man is valid on the psychological plane as well as on the physical and emotional planes.

It is not easy for someone unfamiliar with the so-called Eastern disciplines to get an idea of what this inner work is all about. At the same time, for the person who finds this subject of interest, it is not so complicated and not so far removed from our Western concepts.

Several years ago, a friend who was a ski instructor, a former competitor who had reached an expert level and to whom I had long spoken about my work, personally tested the principles of the figure eight movements I had developed, principles on rooting oneself while moving over a surface. He had followed the classic educational course of the young people who grew up in the area: club competition, ski/study, ski school. His first attempts at working with my new principles were not conclusive, but he worked on them from time to time whenever his busy schedule permitted. One day he arrived at the local tech center buzzing with excitement and a smile that stretched from ear to ear. He exclaimed, "Thias! This Figure Eight Movement! I was simply inside myself and I was not making any extra effort. Incredible! I even had the impression that I was not forcing myself hard enough. I am so used to putting energy into every move, and here I had the impression I was just relaxing into my movements."

"You had the sensation you were not going fast?" I asked him.

"Yes! And I even had it beneath my feet. I knew that I could accelerate if I wanted. I also had the sensation of watching myself."

When a good skier (and a friend, to boot) with more than thirty years of experience comes off the ski slopes with this kind of joy, I am as happy as he is. It is proof that even after so many years of practice we can still make discoveries and progress in our communication with ourselves and with the mountain.

In the beginning, like the majority of my comrades, in my quest for sensation I asserted my tyranny over my body and over the natural environment. I remained anchored in a dominator/dominated relationship: I would dominate the slope or it would dominate me. This cult of the ego imprisoned me in my own world. The better I knew myself internally, the better I knew my physical design; and the better I knew the natural environment and the laws that governed it, the closer I came to achieving the detachment necessary to feel the stance that was perfectly adapted to the situation. This involved abandoning the search for sensation for its own sake—a source of imbalance and dependency—and instead orienting my body, my heart, and my mind toward new perceptions based on respect for myself and for the surrounding environment.

To truly experience the harmony to which, in the final

analysis, we all aspire, I was led to ask myself the following question: In order to attain this blissful state, do I need to abandon the mechanistic attitude and replace it with a kind of mysticism?

A purely mystical attitude refuses to concede anything to the action of the law of cause and effect: in a world where causality is only an illusion, its effect has no meaning. These beliefs compel the mystic to retreat from the world. He seeks only to become one with universal consciousness, to the detriment of individual consciousness. However, despite an inner path that guides him to the total experience of union with the universe, he cannot leave his body without dying. On the other hand, he has no desire to turn outward, for fear of losing contact with the sacred.

A mechanistic attitude gives preference to the law of cause and effect: when I do one thing it will unavoidably lead to another thing. It places causality in the forefront and is consequently conditioned by it. The external has full power. The mechanist reacts to events and thinks that life is simply a matter of conditioned reflexes. He has lost contact with his center. He is entirely focused upon the manipulation of his environment, which he regards as hostile and foreign. In complete contrast to the mystic, he is completely oriented toward the outside; he is obsessed by external stimuli and is severed from his own center.

Faced with this dilemma, I reached the following conclusion: neither one nor the other is completely right or wrong. Once I realized this, I concentrated my efforts on creating connections that would be strong enough to allow both sides of my being to express themselves in unison. The internal and the external both have their place in our actions. A simply mechanistic action disembodies the act; on the opposite extreme, the mystic, in contact with pure awareness, cannot take action without losing touch with his depths.

The impulses that come to life inside me are directed outward.

If I identify with them, I lose myself in the action and scatter my energy, which engenders chains of tension between the internal and the external. A wall separates these two domains for many people. An individual cannot be on both sides at once. However, I have observed that internal centering enables me to perform actions that are much attuned in the world. Centering brings me detachment with regard to the object I desire, the goal to be attained. I observe that, by establishing my awareness in my own heart, I am able to reside in the heart of the action. The term "the inner glide" was born from this observation and this approach.

At the beginning of my training as a ski instructor, I recall being filmed while I skied freely, with an eye to making corrections to my technique. When my turn came to appear on the screen, I did not recognize myself. I was holding myself quite erect, although I had the impression I had been holding my body in a very flexed stance. The gap between what I thought I was doing and what I was really doing was enormous. It was like a smack in the face! I thought I was a much more elegant skier than what the camera captured. I can tell you that, starting the next day, I began following the codified ski instructions to the letter.

This experience taught me that I was not able to place my full trust in my sensations, but it wasn't until later that I grasped why this was so. Our bodies record the experiences of stimuli, as well as how we respond to stumuli. Our muscles inform us on how we are positioned in space in a given moment. The response chosen at any given moment is not always necessarily the best one for a given case, but is rather the one that is most familiar. I felt quite comfortable in the familiar, and thus anything new felt destabilizing.

So, then, how do we evolve? To grasp the essence of this

work, the "glider," whatever his technical level, needs to leave what he knows aside in order to immerse himself in this new approach and feel its nature. The task of letting go of acquired experience is more difficult for the "advanced" skier or snowboarder who, prey to his certitudes, has a tendency to be more rigid than someone who has just begun learning "the basics" and is consequently still full of the desire to learn. The technical level is of secondary importance. It is not necessary to be an expert to feel the glide and to understand the approach I teach in this book. States of limitation can be found on every level. The perfectly attuned gesture is the one that takes into account everything that goes into forming a specific situation. The pure gesture can be realized in a snowplow on a green slope or in a downhill race in the World Cup. In short: the right stance is not reserved for "experts." It involves the way we inhabit our bodies, live its actions, and experience the moment.

I have tried to be as simple as possible in this book. It is designed as a manual, so that you can easily come back to it and find a particular section on which you want to work. I have organized the book into ten chapters. The first chapter helps us situate ourselves in the technical skills we have acquired. Following that, we learn to listen to the surrounding environment, and then to the body, and finally to concentrate on feeling what joins them together.

Simply listening is not enough. Interpretation is equally important, hence the importance of studying the laws of every sport that involves gliding over snow. Then, little by little, we will direct our attention toward learning how to make more effective use of our bodies. As our relationship to our environment changes, we will begin to feel, in flashes, that we are making a transition from combat to harmony. In chapter 6, I assign words to these moments in order to finally reveal a new psychological and emotional structuring that will transform our relationship to the natural environment.

In order to give substance to all of this, I have created gliding *katas,* series of conscious movements that go from the extremely simple to the complex. They will help you to experiment on the slopes with everything that we touch on in this book.

To conclude, we will see how this new approach goes beyond the context of the simple sports activity, is transformed into "an art of gliding," and gradually incorporates itself into our everyday life to where it finally becomes "an art of living." It is this inner journey that I am inviting you to make with me.

CHAPTER 1

The Mechanisms of Gliding and the States of Limitation

To begin we are going to study the various stances we generally adopt to reach our goal—which is to say, getting down the mountain by making a series of turns across the slope (because if we simply go straight down the experience is over too fast!). The stances that I describe here all have one point in common. Each is more or less consciously organized around one or more fixed points inside and outside the body. Our movements are generated based on these fixed points.

Here are these various movement mechanisms.

Stances for Getting Down the Mountain

The Star Glide

The star glide is the stance that is adopted by people who refuse to truly glide. Their fixed point is located at the level of their center of gravity; it is frozen in the back, toward the past moment, the point of lost balance that directly precedes the glide. The belly is blocked; the feet are too far forward. To maintain equilibrium, their hands will raise up and out in front.

The body of the person in the star-glide stance forms a single block, as rigid as the mind of a skier or snowboarder who resists gliding.

$-\overset{\shortmid}{\underset{\shortmid}{-}}-$ = pivotal axis point or fixed point

View from the front   Side view

In the star glide, the rotational axis (or fixed point) is located in back at the level of the center of gravity.

The Metronome Glide

In this stance, contact with the ground is the center for every movement. Like a metronome, the entire body sways from the left to the right and/or from fore to aft in order to find support and an angle leaning over the snow that the glider thinks will assure her control over her movement.

After several turns, the general movement of these skiers takes on greater magnitude to maintain balance; while initially quite enjoyable, this movement mechanism will become a drain on their equilibrium, and these gliders will start struggling to maintain their balance. Their bodies are invaded by muscular tensions and their trajectory becomes dangerous; a skier who uses this method will be forced to lean further in order to brake, and the end result will be a fall. (See the figure at the top of page 20.)

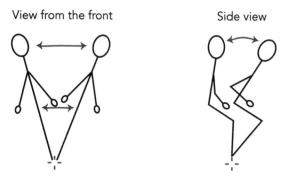

In the metronome glide, the rotational axis (or fixed point) is located at the point where the feet contact the ground.

The Pendulum Glide

The pendulum glide is a movement whose fixed point is the head. The body balances itself from right to left and/or from front to back, like the pendulum of a clock, the head being the clock itself. The movement is generated by a shifting of the pelvis, which in turn pulls the feet. The result is very haphazard. The preciseness of contact with the snow is approximate at best, and muscular tensions are present all over the body.

In the pendulum glide, the rotational axis (or fixed point) is the head.

The Bow Glide

The bow glide is a movement that is centered simultaneously in the head and the feet. The pelvis shifts from right to left and/or from front to back in the image of a bow being drawn. This movement is generally produced by a shift of the pelvis that alters the angle of the ski, snowboard, or skwal on the snow and/or a shift of weight on the board(s) from front to back.

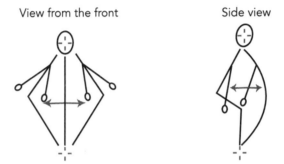

View from the front   Side view

In the bow glide, the rotational axis (or fixed point)
is centered in the head and feet.

This kind of movement engenders a series of muscular tensions, which simultaneously reduces the availability of your physical resources. When bent like a bow, the body will suddenly snap straight (just like a bow) when there is momentary loss of contact with the ground. In other words, the skier will lose his balance.

The Forward Glide

When the glider has grasped that it is better to commit her body to the slope rather than let the slope pull her down it like a vacuum cleaner, she will begin to favor a position toward the front of the board(s), to the detriment of the support on her heel.

Because of this, some skiers will adopt the forward stance as a remedy for every situation. They impose themselves on the slope, sink into it, and maintain this forward stance permanently. We will later see that it is important to not always be "glued to the windshield" at the risk of going through it when high pressure is exerted, such as when skiing a mogul, or at the end of a turn.

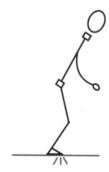

The forward glide, side view

Rotations

There are a multitude of ways to cause the engine to turn. Rotation is the one most often employed.

I need to clarify two details before proceeding further. When I use the word *engine* it can mean skis, snowboard, or skwal. On the other hand, sometimes I will discuss *edge* in the singular, sometimes in the plural. The snowboarder or skwaller will read it in the singular, the skier in the plural. If I have to give specific information regarding a particular "engine," I will explicitly identify whether I am referring to skis, a snowboard, or a skwal.

Rotation on the Back

Rotation on the back of the board(s) is used a great deal by beginning gliders and by the majority of gliders when they begin losing control of the back end of their skis or snowboard or skwal. With the fixed point located on the back of the engine, the glider tries to sweep forward from one side or the other. This movement tends to cause the edges of the board(s) to catch.

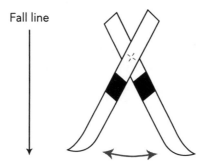

Rotation on the back of the boards is often employed by beginners when they feel themselves losing control.

The Compass

Compass rotation consists of using one foot to support the body's weight while gliding the other foot around with a muscular effort. This movement can be seen quite clearly in some beginning skiers who are trying to learn to snowplow.

Compass rotation is circular movement of one foot around the other.

Forward Rotation

Forward rotation is practiced by more experienced skiers. The fixed point is located on the front of the engine and the skier, snowboarder, or skwaller moves his heel back and forth along the fall line. The control of the trajectory is better than the backward rotation allows. The demand on the muscles is not as great, but the movement is off center; the glider will only use the front of his body and the engine. The weight placed on the back must remain light in order to move without catching an edge.

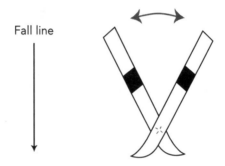

*In forward rotation the fixed point is located
on the front of the board.*

Foot Rotation, or Sweeping

The rotation of the feet, with the middle portion of each foot serving as center, allows the glider to change the direction of the engine rapidly when traveling over a flat surface. (See the following illustration.) The rotation will lose its effectiveness the more the edge of the engine is used, because anchoring the front portion of the engine in the snow will prevent it from rotating.

When starting a turn, it is fairly easy to use muscular effort to flatten the camber of the engine in order to make it pivot. After the board has gone past the fall line, though, the effort expended to make the rotation is no longer serving any purpose, and can

Fall line

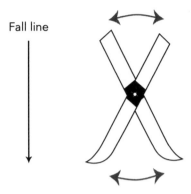

Rotating the feet works to change direction on flat surfaces,
but loses effectiveness when the edge of the engine is employed.

in fact be rather traumatizing. A physical demand is being placed
on the knees and ankles (to twist), while the front of the engine
is sinking deeper into the snow and thus refusing to pivot in the
desired direction. This rotation of the feet is often associated with
a movement of the upper body in the opposite direction.

Rotation of the Thorax

Rotation of the thorax is generally used to rapidly turn the skis
or snowboard or skwal in the other direction and, more exactly,
for keeping the engine from facing into the slope for the least
amount of time possible.

Rotation of the thorax requires at least one fixed point. As a
general rule this will be the feet. At times the pelvis or shoulders
may come in as secondary fixed points (often unconsciously) and
assist in the rotation. For example, for a rotation of the pelvis,
the feet and shoulders can serve as fixed points. Rotation of the
shoulders will likely employ the feet and pelvis as fixed points.

Rotation of the thorax can sometimes be used to accompany a given trajectory. Using it as a mechanism for starting
turns can lead the athlete to experience joint problems because

of the twisting efforts the movement demands. The shoulders can be set in anticipation of a movement, and while the spinal column will accept a shoulder rotation of several degrees, the range of motion of the pelvis is much more limited. Advanced rotation of the pelvis can be traumatizing for the lower joints: the knees and ankles. We will see later that there are mechanics that can produce rotation without relying on the rotation of the joints.

The Mind

Several interpretations of the word *mind* are possible. Rather than defining a word, what I want to discuss here is psychological attitude.

The specifics of any one person's mental functioning results from education and thinking, and is closely connected with will and desire and with the image that person has of him- or herself as well as the image he or she wishes to adopt. Every perception of the outside world passes through the filter of the mind before reaching the individual's consciousness. The mind places a screen between the outside world (the surrounding environment) and the inner world (the persona)—a piece of information coming from the outside is filtered through the mind and is consequently altered. By virtue of the mind's filter, the reality of the situation becomes what one wishes to believe and to see (or not to see).

The world is what it is. Yet, each individual lives in a different world, in his or her own world: that world is the world of the mind, a world that is different from reality, that has a gap between it and the current moment.

...

Our culture and education encourage intellectual development over physical development, and quite often to the detriment of the body and its abilities. The body is far too often manhandled and ignored. Because of this, physical training is often relegated to the background. The mind is stimulated first; the body comes later, if at all. When growing up, the separation between body and mind becomes deeper and the harmony of the body's movements suffers accordingly. The mind imposes its dictatorship. Habits assume full power and are reproduced in a systematic manner, no matter what the situation.

For example, a skier wishes to make a right turn. To do this she commits her head to turning in the direction she wishes to go, just as a pedestrian does. In turn her body pivots, beginning first at the shoulders, then at the pelvis. When the time comes for the legs to follow suit, the skis resist because their edges are anchored in the snow.

If the skis are flat in their movement, the legs can easily make the rotation in their turn. But, if the edges remain anchored in the snow, the skier will lose his balance and fall without further ado. In this situation, the body suffers the will of the head. Following these mental habits in gliding sports can inflict torsions on the body that over the long term will engender physical traumas: the stretching or rupturing of ligaments, slipped vertebral discs, and so forth.

This sequence of movements in initiating a turn is easy to distinguish in the beginner, but it is not reserved to novice skiers. We find this same approach used by a number of high-level skiers. The stance is refined but the movement initiation is the same: turning the head in order to turn the skis. All too often it is the head having its way, and then what pain follows—and what a lack of respect for the body!

In snow-gliding sports the body is located between the natural environment and the will—in other words, between what *is* in the moment and what is translated through the filter of the mind, which makes decisions. If we liken the body to a spring, the mind is a hand that compresses the body, stretches it and twists it, in order to achieve the goals of the mind. Letting go of the spring, ceasing to tyrannize the body and the surrounding environment, is the sole solution for realizing effortless, ecstatic, and safe gliding.

Yes, but how do we do this? To let go of the mind in gliding it is first necessary to study the physical laws that govern our bodies and the environment.

The mental world in which we habitually imprison ourselves does not correspond to the real world, which in this instance is the physical world. The mind can impose its will over the body, but the mind can never change the rules that shape the world to which the body (and the mind) are subject.

When I make myself receptive to hearing what my body is saying, it will inform me of its position in the space it is occupying. When I know the physical laws applicable to skiing or other sports that involve gliding over snow, I can purposely place my body here or there, wherever the function of the effort dictates. The action is no longer simply wishing this or that result by turning my head in the direction that I want to go, but being able to attain the goal through the application of the fundamental laws pertaining to the physical act of gliding.

The person who is aware of this mechanism gradually sheds the mental despotism that bullies the body. The fundamental transformation is internal. By abandoning the tyranny over and repression of his or her body, the glider opens the doors of perception and expression within.

Here is a small and extremely interesting exercise that illustrates the power of the mind in gliding.

Facing the fall line on an easy slope for you, make a few wide-angle traverses across the trail. Then, at the completion of a turn, gradually point the board(s) uphill until you come to a complete stop. Chances are that you were able to accomplish this easily. (If you are not at a level of proficiency yet that will let you perform this wide-angle traverse down the slope, you can do the same exploration using a snowplow turn.)

Now do the same exercise, but this time with your eyes closed. What happens?

With your eyes closed, you will have a tendency to fall uphill when you come to a stop. Why? The glider traditionally leads the body with the head, facing in the direction of the desired objective. At the moment of coming to a stop, what little centripetal force he was subjected to disappears. Leaning uphill without the aid of the eyes to warn of the impending stop will cause the glider to lose his balance.

Now practice the exercise again with your eyes closed, but this time paying attention to the pressure at the soles of your feet. You will experience balance in a more refined manner. Imbalances are corrected automatically. With this first experience in your body, you are now heading to what I call the physical glide.

Toward the Physical Glide

The physical glide can be described as the glide in which every movement originates in the body, with the mind playing only a supporting role.

Like every body that possesses mass (weight), the human body has a center of gravity. This center is located approximately three fingers' width above the navel in front of the spinal column. The body's mass is organized around this center. When a human being is standing, the projection of the body's mass onto the ground passes through the soles of the feet. This standing posture is supported by the body's skeletal structure and muscle tone in opposition to the gravitational attraction of Earth. There is a relationship of dynamic equilibrium between the Earth and the human, and it is our feet that inform us about the quality of that relationship at every moment. The human body and the Earth can only be one in an action by virtue of this permanent attunement.

We have two modes of behavior available to us. The mind-dominated mode is *wanting* to do it: the mind desires to make an action, and the body suffers that tyranny. For example, I desire to turn my skis without taking into account that my edges are anchored in the snow. I use force on my joints to achieve my desired result—and there will be inevitable consequences in my body's well-being. The other mode of behavior is *being able* to do it. In this physically dominated mode the body can bring the head where the head wishes to go, if the head listens to the body and respects the physical laws that govern movement. If I want to turn my skis, I must first free them from the grip of the snow (by setting them flat, for example). My task will be greatly simplified, my movement more efficient and graceful, and my body well cared for in the moment.

When the intellect is stronger than the laws that govern movement, then your true goals in movement will never be achieved—or if they are, it will only be at the price of real physical torture! Whether you are a beginner or an expert glider, no one escapes this rule.

The three stages of integration

1. In the beginning is the mental glide. I direct myself toward the goal to be reached (physically) with my head; for better or worse, my body tries to follow the movement that has been imposed on it.

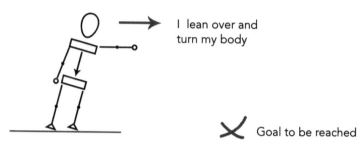

I lean over and turn my body

Goal to be reached

2. Going in reverse. Placing my body's weight to the left in order to go right, lowering myself in order to go up . . . I am beginning to use my body to reach the goal but I am still in a dualistic relationship between the mind and body. The forces work against each other.

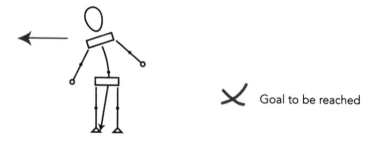

Goal to be reached

3. Centering in the physical glide. The glider ceases to project himself into stances and psychologically places himself in "the axis that causes the wheel to turn"—the body's center of gravity, the center of movement. Now the body and the surrounding environment can unite.

The soles of the feet inform the glider about the position of the body's center of gravity in space. The connections that are created between the feet and the gravity center encourage the shedding of muscular tensions that no longer serve any purpose. The only muscular tensions remaining are those that are necessary to maintain the balance of the glider's stance at each particular moment. The body's mass is projected over the feet, in the location that will best realize the desired effect. The mind's will to achieve an objective gives way to the body's intelligent use of gravity, which produces the desired result.

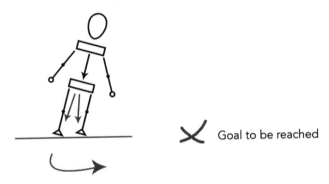

Goal to be reached

In summary, the attraction or repulsion of the object of our attention places us in an antagonistic relationship. The more we strive toward our goal, the more it becomes mechanically inaccessible. The will to unite with the object of desire is not enough; so, by a reversing of mental and physical functioning, I head away from the desired object in order to reach it. The result is already quite a bit better, but the mechanisms used still belong to the reactive mode. In the third stage, physical glide, we realize the ability to go beyond the dualist relationship. We consciously experience the physical laws through our body, the source of harmonious movement. In the physical heart of the action, all that remains is the application of the physical laws governing movement in the instant in order to reach the goal that has been set. I put myself in the right place at the right time, gravity does its work, and the goal is achieved.

CHAPTER 2

In Tune with the Surrounding Environment

To find his location and to move about the Earth, man identified the four cardinal points and invented the compass. The Chinese, however, believed there were five cardinal points, the fifth point being the actual physical place on Earth where the individual happens to be at the moment. That is the source point.

I mention this to point out that, for the purpose of getting an overall view of a situation and in order to position herself effectively within the environment, the human being begins by gathering her energies into her body. To be attuned to the surrounding environment, it is of fundamental importance to create an emptiness within in order to receive the information specific to a situation.

In this chapter we will explore how to place ourselves in the environment with regard to the stimuli requesting our attention and how to manage those stimuli.

The Four Physical Spheres of Influence

Thanks to the laws of gravity, every object—including human beings, snowflakes, and the Earth—is organized around a center. These units attract each other in proportion to their individual masses—i.e., man is drawn toward the Earth. This is the law of attraction.

Often the visual experience of an environment will produce psychological, physical, and emotional attractions or repulsions in an individual; we experience the beauty of a spot, or dizzying space. These attractions and repulsions have a destabilizing effect on us, causing us to think less lucidly, less clearly.

We can classify the physical environment of the glider into four different spheres of influence:

1. The personal space: my body.
2. The kinesphere: the space of my immediate action. It is in relationship to this space that I construct each of my physical actions. The size of this space is proportional to the speed of my movement.
3. The visual space: the space I grasp through looking.
4. The larger world to which I belong: the Earth.

The body is subject to the same physical laws as nature. In order to avoid being alarmed or disturbed by the visual space, I concentrate on my body: gathering my energy into my body, making contact with the Earth with the soles of my feet, and connecting with the Earth to form a good grounding. The glider aware of this will continue to perceive the space of the immediate action and the visual space with his eyes, without either of those stimuli producing a destabilizing effect on his balance.

Centered in his body, the skier, the snowboarder, the skwaller moves through the visual space by compromising with the space of the action, which is changing constantly. The glider who experiences the space of immediate action as if he were beneath a clear glass cheese dome cannot truly connect with his surrounding environment. It is only when he pulls his head "out of the bag" of his horizontal reading of the world (where information is perceived sequentially) that he begins to view himself as part of a greater whole.

The space that has the gravity center of the body as its zero point is represented by three axes:

- The first, which is vertical, symbolically connects the sky to the center of the Earth, but primarily represents the axis of terrestrial attraction that passes through the body. A good physical verticality is obtained when the correctly aligned skeleton frees the muscles from useless tension.
- The second, which is horizontal, is in the background and represents time, with its zero point the here and now. This point is the source of every action.
- The third represents the space to the left and the space to the right.

Every element of the mountain is drawn toward one point: the center of the Earth, the meeting point and point of unity. The verticality experienced internally, in balance and in a sense of being rooted, engenders a feeling of unity with the surrounding elements. This unity brings serenity.

Horizontality separates: there is me and the solution on the outside, located in the near future. Verticality unites: in the heart of the action, connected to Earth, I become one body with the environment through the Earth.

The glider enters a space that involves him physically. Detachment from first the environment and then from his body is necessary to fully comprehend and appreciate the four spheres of influence. Being detached does not mean being absent. In order to be an observer of the situation and each of its component elements, the glider places himself at the top of an imaginary pyramid whose base is his body and his board(s), the configuration of the terrain, and the physical laws governing bodies in motion. One must be constantly attentive to all three if balance is to be maintained. The stool stands up because it has three feet. If one is removed, it will fall down. A glider who overlooks one of these components will disrupt the balance of his movement.

From the relationship of observer/observed, which is essentially divisive and that separates all units into two and maintains duality, the glider makes the transition to an all-inclusive relationship in consciousness—the source of unity—and consequently provides ease in movement down the slope.

This won't just happen by suggestion, or because you want it to. You must learn to recognize the signs, and to do this there is no substitute for experience.

Whatever the case may be, good skiers and other gliding enthusiasts, not to mention extremely good athletes from other disciplines, have acquired gestures through repetition and training and then imposed themselves on their environment in much the same way they have imposed this training on their bodies. But what can be said about the quality of this relationship?

Attuning the body with its environmental context provides the athlete with a sum total of internal pieces of information—pressures; feelings of lightness, relaxation, contraction—and external information—the condition of the trail, the quality of the snow, the trajectory of the slope, the location of dips and bumps. This information is managed via the knowledge of the physical phenomena specific to gliding sports and their implications for the body and its movements. Understanding the physical laws and using them consciously opens new avenues of expression and movement for the skier, snowboarder, and skwaller.

CHAPTER 3

Attuning to Your Body

Respecting the Way Your Joints Are Designed

The human body is designed in such a way that each joint possesses a certain number of possible movements, so that once they are all working together, the body can meet the demands for every desired movement. With a gliding engine beneath one's feet, contact with the ground changes—the pressures on the ground increase or are reduced. Constraints in the joints can have a traumatic effect if the skier, snowboarder, or skwaller has not integrated the new data specific to the activity.

The glider must first and foremost be attuned to his body and respect its limitations if he wishes to stay safe and enjoy the use of his body for a long time. A person gliding over snow, by whatever means, generally moves through a series of turns down the mountain, and subjects his body to a large number of super-high pressures in the process. The rotations of the tibias (the long bone of the foreleg) over the feet, or the pelvis over the tibias, combined with these very high pressures are extremely damaging to the joints and cartilage. Furthermore, a body that is twisted like a screw will be subjected to involuntary unscrewing if the gliding engine loses its anchoring in the snow while, for example, negotiating a curve.

A femur and a tibia or a tibia and ankle/foot should maintain their alignment. A lateral thrust of the knees leads to trauma if it is not combined with compression. Engaging an edge will necessarily be combined with bending the lower limbs. A simple test to verify this is to push the knees sideways when standing upright on a flat surface. The angle between the ankles and the ground is reduced. Do the same thing with a good compression of the ankles, knees, and hips and note the difference. The tibia remains in alignment with the ankle and foot, the femur in alignment with the knee and tibia. Only the top of the femur bone revolves, at the hip joint, the housing that is designed for precisely this action. Joint function and alignment is respected. It is the unobstructed joints that can fulfill their role as distributors of shifting pressures in the event of terrain change.

As for the chest, it is permissible for the shoulders to move independent of the hips, but the shoulders should never initiate a turn. The shoulders can accompany, and even prolong or accelerate a rotation, provided that the edges of the engine are not caught in the snow, but that is all.

In each of these movements, the glider should refrain from pushing her joints to their maximum range. Keeping a margin of safety will allow for unforeseen events, for unexpected forces to be absorbed. In the basic stance, the midrange compression of the ankles, knees, and hips of the glider will guarantee a good flexion or extension in responding effectively to external demands.

The Foot: Sensor and Information Provider

Let's begin with a simple exercise that will help us become aware of our mechanics. Starting in a traverse, execute a long, shallow turn with your eyes closed, ending by turning uphill. Practice this accompanied by others so as to avoid accidents. This exercise will most likely demonstrate that your perceptions are greatly disturbed, causing some to lose their balance when making the turn uphill. Most people will lose their balance when they come to a stop. Sight and the mind are closely associated. This imbalance is evidence of an essentially mental approach to your snow sport. The head is carrying the body toward the inside of the turn. The desire to make a turn has taken the lead over the body's inherent knowing. The physical means for achieving the turn successfully have been relegated to a secondary plane.

Start the exercise again, but this time focus your awareness on the soles of your feet. The difference is enormous: you will likely not lose your sense of balance. If you want to perform a test that will have more credibility, ask a friend to perform the same exercise without giving him or her the solution and watch what happens.

In this kind of exploration, the appropriate perception of how the body should respond to the change in terrain can only be made by the feet and, more specifically, by the pressure placed on the ground by the soles of the feet. The sensations that we receive through the soles of the feet inform us about our verticality.

The foot, the part of the body that is farthest from the head, is often overlooked as a source of physical information, and yet what we need to know concerning our equilibrium comes from our base: our feet.

The placement that we adopt in this exercise is dictated by the body's center of gravity, which responds directly to the information provided by the feet. The feet are like probes that read the pressure the body places on the ground. The gravity center and the feet are closely linked to assure the balance of the whole.

Our feet connect us to the ground; they are our "mobile" roots.

CHAPTER 4

Connecting with the Ground

Putting Down Roots

The roots permit the tree to hold itself upright and resist the attacks of the wind. The larger the tree, the greater its needs will be for good roots that are large and go deep.

For the human being who is standing up, the roots are the upholding surface in contact with the ground: the soles of the feet. As this surface is not extendable, the human being has two options for attaining greater stability: spreading her feet and/or bending lower to the ground.

In order to improve her sense of feeling rooted, the skier makes contact with the ground by the soles of her feet. To do this, starting from a standing stance, she allows her head and shoulders to stand over her pelvis *through* the center of gravity, with her abdomen relaxed within the pelvis. The belly is not sucked in to form a hollow, nor is the back rounded.

Having formed a single unit, the body stands in a relaxed pose over the soles of the feet. The skier (or snowboarder or skwaller) should not be leaning too far forward or back, nor too much to either side; the body's weight should be balanced equally over both feet, with a sense of being centered in the relaxation of your muscles. The centers of your feet are open

and making contact with the ground. This center, located in the plantar arch, is the junction point and distribution point for the body mass over the whole foot. The centers of the feet, while not in direct contact with the ground, form a direct connection between the body's center of gravity and the ground. Awakening these centers is a fundamental step before making any action. At all times, they are the source point for equillibrium.

In order to better feel what is happening beneath our feet, we bring our mind to a state of calm through slow, deep breathing. To facilitate the engagement of contact with our feet, we can create a slight shifting of balance from one foot to the other. The pressure on the ground increases, our perceptions awaken, and—little by little—the balancing movement disappears, to be replaced by simple and direct contact with the ground by both feet. A slight bending of the joints is necessary; this brings stability and relaxation.

The feet centers open when contact with the ground has been established. This conscious perception of the ground creates a strong bond, which is a source of equilibrium and sequenced movements.

Achieving this sensation of being rooted to the ground is closely connected to the basic stance of any gliding activity. Preformed boots facilitate the flexion of the ankles. Combining this flexion with the bending of the knees and hips reinforces contact with the ground. In the kick transmission on the edges, the rigidity of the material provides compensation for the absence of direct contact with the ground by the center of the foot. The points of pressure through the soles of the feet should remain in contact with the ground throughout the duration of a linked series of movements. If our body mass moves forward to placement over our toes, the heels will come off the ground. This is true in reverse as well: when the body's weight moves over the heels, the toes come off the ground. In both cases the centers of the feet, and balance, are lost.

Placement over the soles of the feet is fundamental but cannot be separated from the placement of the pelvis, the abdomen, the shoulders, the spinal column; breathing; and presence in the moment. We dissect things even though we know the human body is an indivisible whole. Intervening at one spot brings about changes to the entire body.

By accepting the stance for what it is, with complete physical and mental relaxation, you will reinforce your sense of being rooted, and all the movements you make will be balanced.

Centering

Psychologically speaking, human beings are rarely in the center of the movement when skiing or snowboarding or skwalling. Their center of interest lies outside. The simple fact of wishing to possess what they do not have, or to be where they are not in this moment, brings about an internal rift, a division that is a source of imbalance.

When he is centered in his body, the skier can communicate with the surrounding environment in a more natural and objective manner. The movement down the slope is born from inner excitement—not from an external attraction or repulsion. Focusing on a center that lies outside the self places the body on a secondary plane. The body is no longer the subject; it has become a peripheral object. When you are centered within yourself, within your center of gravity, you organize your body mass around this point; for example, a good lateral thrust over one foot will create a strong liaison between that foot and the center of gravity. As a skier you place yourself within the axis of the equilibrium and are constantly rebalancing the scales

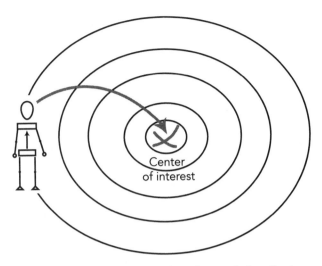

For most skiers (and snowboarders and skwallers)
the center of interest lives outside themselves.

in accordance with the terrain, the desired trajectory, and the mechanical effect that you want to achieve on the snow. Your placement, and consequently the projection on the ground of the center of gravity, are governed by you as a skier in accordance with physical laws and the effect desired, produced by the engine.

Being centered within your body means inhabiting it permanently—feeling it, relaxing it, and grasping the information it is providing you every second. Centering precedes and accompanies the action. The skier then carries out his actions by remaining detached from objects, objectives, and results.

To do in order to have, to do for a purpose other than the doing itself, creates a dependence that is both destructuring and has a harrowing effect on one's state of mind. For example, to wish to possess the end of the turn at the moment the turn has been initiated creates a tension in the body directed toward the goal, with the effect that the body is placed in a stance that is not adapted to the actual moment but to the moment that is being anticipated.

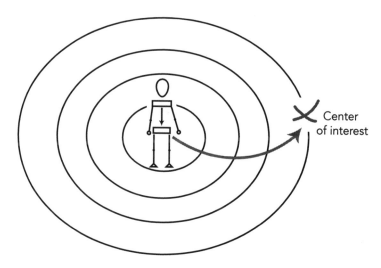

When the center of interest lies inside the movement,
the movement is effortless and effective.

We are ceaselessly outside of ourselves, dragged along by the incessant flow of attractions and repulsions from the outside world. As a general rule, we leave our bodies to head toward a center of interest that is external to us. When my entire body is stretched taut, projected toward the outside, I am displaying my preference for the external; I am seeking to possess something. But this goal is separate from me and automatically places me in an internal conflict: feeling torn, separate from, off center.

To put myself in the correct stance, a reversal is called for. Aware that the center of interest is outside of me, I remain, despite everything, anchored within my body, the only reality, the here and now, the sole support to the realization of my goal.

So what can I do to realize my goal? What resources do I have at my disposal?

What I utilize for the achievement of a purpose is my body, my mind, and the surrounding elements. I realize a series of turns down the slope without desire and with detachment, always working out of the present moment, little by little, while seeking to maintain my anchoring in my body and the equilibrium of every instant.

Wishing to possess the world and being possessed by it is the danger. When we free our grip on the world, we are already liberating ourselves to some extent from its grip on us.

The Center of Gravity

We can compare our center of gravity to the hub of a wheel around which its mass is organized. When the wheel turns, the movement of the whole thing is harmonious because the geometric center and the center of gravity have become as one. Once the whole is centered properly, it can give birth to balanced movement.

The center of gravity is at the center of the wheel. The center of gravity when in projection is at the feet.

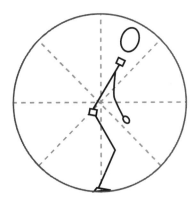

When the body is balanced in projection down the mountain,
the center of gravity is at the feet.

Let's now pick a point on one spoke of the turning wheel and place the gravity center of the skier on that spot. The point will be subject to a variety of movements, going up and down, back and forth. This point has a mass that is large enough to put the wheel off center. The rotating movement of the whole will organize itself around a new center. Geometrically speaking, it will be off center and create a new movement outside of the wheel's physical center. When a wheel that is off center gains speed, it will eventually no longer be turning round. Loss of contact and extremely high pressures follow each other in succession.

The same holds true for the human being in movement. Every movement is organized, in a more or less conscious manner, in accordance with the placement of the center of gravity. Quite often, the center of gravity is not the center of the movement. Suddenly, the entire body is reacting, compensating for the loss of balance through a series of muscular tensions that are all detrimental to the smooth and unobstructed movement of the wheel. A succession of inseparable phenomena will follow from this off-centered movement: points of extremely high pressure alternating with loss of contact, acceleration, and slowing down.

This example does not imply that the gravity center should be motionless or static. Quite the contrary. It should only be at the heart of the action. Centered within his center of gravity, the skier or snowboarder establishes a connection with the centers of his feet, which themselves are in contact with the plane of reference: the ground. This centering within the body permits the skier or snowboarder to structure himself internally, to gradually acquaint himself with and inhabit his body, his "inner architecture." He directs his thought inward, inside his body, toward what is the base of balanced movement, the source point. It is the strong point for every action.

The action is born in this point and radiates outward toward the extremities of the body, then toward the elements that make up the present situation.

Let's go back to the example of the wheel. If the skier places her center of gravity on a spoke of the wheel, her action will consist of movements that go back and forth, up and down, and she will inevitably enter a process of reactive movements intended to maintain an impossible balance—impossible because it is off centered. In this case the center of movement lies outside of her and she finds herself the prisoner of a center that she has created but cannot control.

This happens quite a bit with those who use the "leap-frog" method of skiing when negotiating a steep slope, which is to say they hop from one support to the other. Gradually the movement takes on greater dimension and is no longer controllable or effective, thereby necessitating the skier to stop in order to break this process of increasingly compromised equilibrium.

Our feet and our hands inform us about our bodies' placement in space at every moment. The tensions in our body indicate if the gesture is adapted correctly to the situation and if our body mass is correctly distributed.

CHAPTER 5

Toward More Effective Use of Your Body

Skiing and other such snow sports are about gliding; they are not about clinging on for dear life.

Throughout this book, I often refer to the physical laws and how to use them. They are the foundation for every move we make. The most refined skier can do nothing without them; he experiences them through the intermediary of his body, through constant monitoring of phenomena, and a "losing of the self." The skier (or any other glider) becomes the conscious channel of the great ballet of the physical laws and expresses him- or herself on the snow through and thanks to those laws.

The Simplified Principles of Gliding over Snow

In order to glide in an aware and effective manner, it is necessary to understand the physical laws that influence our movements over the snow. I am presenting here, in a fairly simple fashion, the physical phenomena that are the most important. We should know them absolutely, as they have an influence on each and every one of our actions.

The quality of glide over the snow is influenced by several factors:

- The strength of the Earth's attraction
- Minimal friction
- Resistance to the penetration
- The gradient of the slope
- The type of snow-gliding engine used

Let's observe the reactions of a gliding engine placed on a groomed trail and subjected to several experiments involving shifting the placement of the body mass.

Facing the slope, the engine flat

First, let's place the engine on a groomed trail facing the slope, with the engine flat. The mass is centered toward the back of the board.

Now let go. What happens? The back wishes to move forward to the front; the heavy tries to go in front of the light.

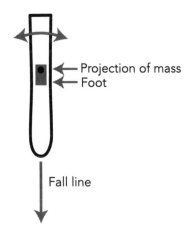

Shifting the weight forward, the back follows the front. The heavy pulls the light behind it.

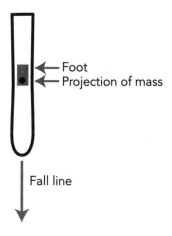

Going across the slope, the engine flat

This time let's take an engine, hook a weight on the front of it, and position it so it is lying flat on the snow and directly across a trail that is absolutely smooth. Let go of the board. What happens?

The engine begins to glide laterally while simultaneously the tip of the engine dives deeper and deeper into the fall line. The engine will continue past the fall line before coming back to it, after oscillating back and forth to stabilize itself in a glide down the slope.

Because the front is heavier, it provides the direction that the back of the engine will follow.

I need to make a certain clarification here: when one speaks of an engine lying flat for a glider, it is a practical term that defines the angle of the engine on the snow so that the skier or snowboarder can go into a sideslip (for this exercise). It is quite obvious that an engine that stays *completely* flat during a side-slip will get snagged by the snow and turn over.

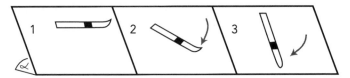

The trajectory of a "flat" engine, with weight on the front

Let's repeat the same exercise, this time with the weight hung on the heel side of the engine. It will dive down the slope but this time the back will go first.

The trajectory of a "flat" engine, with weight on the back

If we could, in the absolute sense, merge the two parts of this experiment, the engine would simply turn as the weight was transferred from front to back. The rotating movement takes place in the fall line, with very little lateral deviation, because the edges aren't catching the snow.

This experiment shows us that a change of direction can be achieved without actually rotating the body. The starting point of the shift is in the transfer of weight. The change of the engine's direction is due to the play of the placement of the mass that a glider can easily realize with his body.

Lateral sideslip by engaging the edges

Let's imagine a glider on a very steep, smooth slope, making a lateral sideslip with his engine flat. He is hurtling downhill at a fast speed. To brake or stop himself, all he needs to do is increase the degree the edge is engaged while remaining poised above the center of his feet.

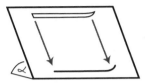

Braking by intensifying the degree of edge on the snow while remaining centered over the feet

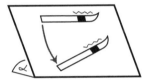

The effects of shifting the weight to the front when braking

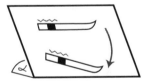

The effects of shifting the weight to the back when braking

If the glider shifts his weight over the front of his feet at the time he is engaging his edges, he will create extremely high pressure on the front of the engine, the front end of the engine will dive into the snow, and at the same time his skis will come free from the surface in the back on the downhill side due to his weak anchoring. The opposite effects will occur when the glider shifts his weight to the back when engaging his edges.

Expecting the direction of a curve

The gliding engines have thin, grooved edges to facilitate steering through curves. A simple push on the edges draws the skier into a curve. By combining this push on the edge with the pressure exerted by the skier's mass, often by way of a compressed muscular movement, the engine increasingly curves inward.

View from the front

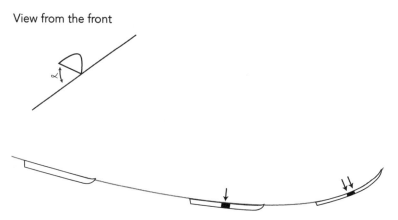

Pushing on the edge of the engine draws the glider into a curve.

We can combine these different mechanisms to descend a slope. The rules are the same for all: beginners and seasoned skiers. To glide effectively, keep the skis or other engine flat on the snow as much as possible, paradoxically even when more of your weight is shifted to the edges. This allows the glider more freedom when moving into curves.

The glider naturally wants to "anchor himself" in the snow by encouraging edging. Consequently, he must always be mindful to extend toward the *minimal* angle necessary to produce the desired curve, halfway between losing the edge and anchoring.

During a run with a carving turn, the phase of entering the

slope should be done on the front of the middle of the foot, and controlling the turn should be governed by the back of the foot, in order to be able to set the engine flat at any moment. This will modify the initial course of the engine without using effort in rotation or creating too extreme an angle when edging.

It is quite obvious that the glider can steer his engine throughout a carving turn by keeping his weight toward the front, but the moment that a high pressure is applied, such as muscular compression, the directional effect will take on too much magnitude and lead to too sharp a turn of the engine, propelling the glider too far forward. In contrast, shifting the body's weight too far back on the foot will encourage the skis or board to float in the flat phases. It will also result in difficulty entering the curve on a steep slope, followed by periods of imbalance on the back end when very high pressure is encountered in the second part of the curve, causing the engine to accelerate and the back end to lose balance.

Here is an image that can help us grasp how to modify or maintain a course most effectively. An engine gliding over snow behaves somewhat like a sailplane without a rudder, one in which the passengers can be moved from front to back or from one wing to the other to change the trajectories. The nose and tail of the sailplane are equivalent to the tip and tail of the ski, and the wings are the edges. The center of the plane is the center of the foot.

If the passengers move toward the front, the plane will make a nose dive; if the passengers move toward the back it will pull upward; to either wing and it will glide to the left or right. By placing the passengers in the front and over the right wing, the nose of the plane will dive while soaring toward the right. Conversely, placing the passengers on the back and over the right wing, the back end of the machine will go down on the right side, with

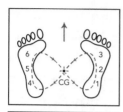

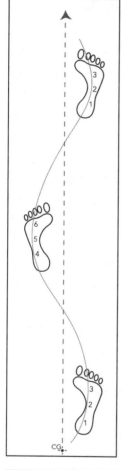

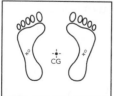

the nose pointing to the left. This example makes it easy to see that the direction of the machine changes based on the placement of mass.

The same is true for the engine gliding over snow. The course of the engine can change without rotating the body or anchoring the edges in the snow. Like the imagined sailplane, the engine free of the snow's grip becomes governable, by the simple placement of mass. Learning the proper, simple transfer of weight on the feet is the essence of the Figure Eight Movement, my basic teaching in centered, efficient gliding.

The Figure Eight Movement

The movements of our body's weight on the level of the feet will indicate to us, if we are attuned, our body's placement in space.

Let's begin our exploration of the Figure Eight Movement by investigating what pressures we experience at the soles of the feet during walking. The walking step begins with a displacement of the body's mass over the front of the feet.

Walking steps begin with a placement of the heel; the foot unrolls toward the toes (CG = center of gravity).

Then the walker puts one foot forward, places her heel, unrolls the foot down toward the front, transfers the mass to the other foot, and starts over. A slight lateral swaying of the body's mass facilitates the transfer of weight from one side to the other.

In observing the sequence of pressures over the plantar arch, a figure eight movement will appear. (A wink of the eye from the author in passing, a horizontal eight is the symbol of infinity and perpetual movement.)

In contrast to the walker, the skier when making a turn unrolls the foot from the toes to the heel. In fact, at the beginning of the turn, the skier seeks support from the front of the foot, which encourages the engine to enter the slope, then gradually the dominant support moves to the middle and finally to the back of the foot while descending the slope, until the turn has been completed.

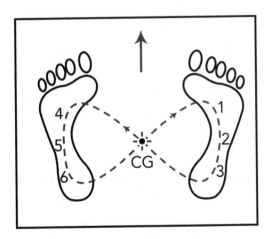

A skier unrolls the foot from toes to
heels (CG = center of gravity).

The eight represents the trajectory of the projection of mass beneath the feet.

Careful! During the glide the fore and aft pressure points on the sole of the foot are closer to the center point of the foot than they are when walking, because anchoring by the center of the foot can only occur if the front and back of the foot are in constant contact with the Earth. The "step" therefore occurs over a much smaller surface than is involved in walking.

The most difficult part of learning the Figure Eight Movement for skiing and gliding is learning to maintain contact with the Earth during the transfer of weight from back to front. A great number of gliders play with their mass, more for creating a way to push their weight up from their board(s) and thus encouraging the movement of the engine (or the body) from right to left, than for creating judicious placement of the body mass over the engine and initiating a natural rotation of the whole. Pushing one's weight from the engine uproots the skier and will cause a loss of balance.

To the fore/aft movement of the mass is connected a lateral movement corresponding to edging in all its subtleties. The lateral movement can be produced by two different mechanics that can be combined or not, as the skier wishes: a lateral and general inclination of the body and a lateral movement of the knees. The juxtaposition of the fore/aft movements and the lateral movements produce a rotational movement of the projection of the body's mass around the center of the foot.

At every moment, the center of the foot and the point of principal support are applying pressure on the sole. Once the center of the foot loses contact with the Earth, the root is cut—the skier loses her balance and falls back into her old mechanisms.

The Figure Eight Movement requires less energy because the glider is in a state of constant balance and does not look like a kangaroo bounding from one support to the other.

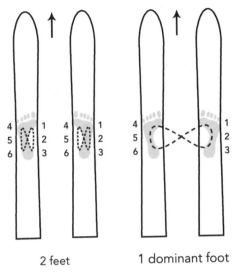

2 feet   1 dominant foot

The Figure Eight Movement on skis

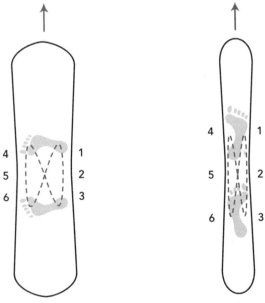

The Figure Eight Movement
on snowboard

The Figure Eight Movement
on skwal

Rotational movement around the center of the foot. 0 is the center of the foot. The ╱ represents the zone of the greatest pressure applied by the weight of the body. Other combinations are possible, but what is important is the omnipresent contact at the 0 point (the center of the foot), associated with one of the points of the Figure Eight Movement.

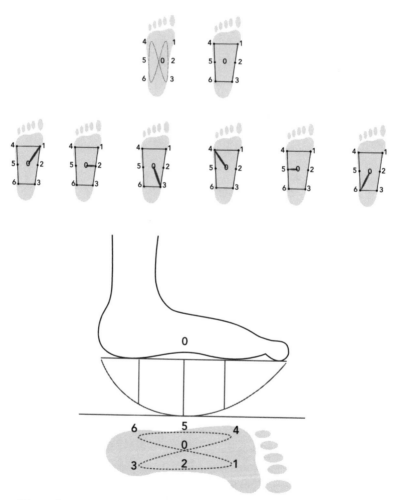

To go from one point to another, the 0 point works like a ball and socket joint, not as an axis of horizontal rotation.

The (Non) Effort in Rotation

Making a turn over snow is achieved by a series of placements of your body over your board(s), causing the whole to pivot.

If the glider initiates a rotational movement of his body (or part of it) with a muscular effort, this rotational movement must be halted at the end of the turn, then oriented in the other direction, and so on: I project a movement, I stop it, I project another movement, and so forth. What an effort! The body suffers the distress produced by rotational movements. Rotational movement over an engine still anchored on the edge creates microtraumas of the joints and, over the long term, pain and disability.

In skiing, for example, when I want to go toward the right, I turn my feet in that direction. As long as my skis are flat on the snow, the movement is tolerated, but things get complicated when I turn on the edges. My body precedes my skis in this rotational movement and pressure is applied to my joints, without it causing any larger of a turn than the one my skis are prepared to make.

For a rotational movement to be effective and not cause physical damage, the engine should be free of the snow's grip—in other words, it should be flat. Before attempting to integrate rotational movements into your skiing experience, seek to use the physical phenomena connected to gravity and the distinctive qualities of your chosen snow engine.

The example cited above is the typical example of the mental turn: the head wants it and the body suffers for it. The mind wants everything, and it wants it right now.

By applying the laws of physics, the glider can emerge from this dynamic imposed by the mind. The turn no longer finds its initiation in the effort required to rotate, but in the conscious application of the physical laws that cause the skis to rotate. The body and the surrounding environment are as one. It is no longer a case of: "I am fighting in a hostile environment to achieve my goals," but "I am making a compromise with a natural element in respect of the laws that govern it and those that govern my body when making a gliding movement."

By studying the physical laws of the glide, the placements of mass that will lead to a turn become obvious. The concept of nonrotation takes on its meaning.

We can observe that a large number of gliding sport enthusiasts, of every level, use the effort required to pivot even more when they are in trouble—when they are making the turn too late, or their body's weight is too far back on the skis. We cannot draw a technique out of it, even if it should be acknowledged that a rotational movement as a reflexive action can pull the skier or snowboarder out of a bad spot. The operational effort of rotation should only be used as a last resort, and preferably only when the skis are lying flat over the snow.

The ideal rotation of the skis is achieved as a consequence of a series of positioning of the body's mass, and therefore is in respect of the design of the body's joints.

Compression and Extension

In traditional skiing technique, compression and extension are used to encourage lifting the body's weight from the skis, for the purpose of facilitating the rotation you want the boards to make.

With the Figure Eight Movement technique (and thus the utilization of physical laws), the lifting of the body's weight by muscular effort loses its usefulness. Nevertheless, compression/extension remains an interesting mechanism and one that has its uses, but for other purposes.

When adopting the base position of the Figure Eight Movement, the glider is semiflexed and relaxed, with her spine inclining slightly forward. When the glider produces a slight extension in the axis of the spinal column, she will perceive a movement of her mass forward over the soles of her feet. If she produces a compression along the same axis, the projection of her mass will shift behind her. If either the compression or the extension is a large movement, the glider will lose her rooting and prompt a series of muscular tensions to compensate for her loss of balance.

Extension causes the glider's stance to lean toward the front, which when the skis or snowboard are brought into flat contact with the surface of the snow, will make the skier (or snowboarder) lean into the slope. Extension corresponds to the first part of the turn. Conversely, compression corresponds to the second part of the turn. If the gliding engine is flat, the mass placed aft will pull the glider into rotation. Compression facilitates setting the edges in a way that supports braking, lateral movements, and other directional changes. In Figure Eight Movement technique, the mechanism of compression/extension is utilized at the same moment as in traditional technique, but with one important difference: it is not used as a means to lift one's weight from the skis.

I have intentionally left out discussion of the lateral angles in order to simplify the explanation.

In the Figure Eight Movement technique, we are using two phases—extension, then compression—with the desire of moving toward maintaining a constant distribution of weight over the snow throughout the length of the curve in order to improve the skier's looseness and balance. The turn has two phases. In the first phase the weight of the body is in front of the center of the feet; in the second phase it is behind the center of the feet.

In the control of a long turn using the edge as support, if

the skier, for example, wishes to change trajectory for a shorter radius, a simple flattening of the engine will cause a gravity-produced pivot. Because the mass is behind the center of the foot, the heel digs into the slope and pivots the body. To stop the movement the skier has two solutions at his disposal: to recenter his mass over the center of his feet, or pick the edge up a little to regain the directional steering of the ski. As you will note, no volitional rotational action has been called for here.

On the fore/aft plane as on the vertical plane, the more refined movements and those of less range offer the benefits of less effort and more efficiency.

Matter changes, and so do techniques. Everyone watches and seeks to understand the technique of the other but every individual is different, and acts and reacts differently when faced with various situations. Everyone has balance and energy within. There is a time to abandon one's certainties, a time to listen, feel, and connect with the elements, a time for the profound being inside each one of us to simply be.

The Double Figure Eight Movement

On skis or on a skwal, the Figure Eight Movement of the center of gravity combines two movements: lateral movement and vertical movement. Lateral movement allows us to more or less shift weight from one foot to another. This movement is practically nonexistent on a run taking small turns facing the slope. Once the body repositions itself away from the fall line, then movement can take birth. Vertical movement, meanwhile, facilitates the balanced shifting of the body's mass fore and aft.

To facilitate the mastering of this Figure Eight Movement, you can accompany the movement of your center of gravity with an exaggerated duplication of it with your hands. Choose

a gentle slope that is not too fast and that offers a wide turning radius. Once you have gotten the movement in your head, do it without the help of your hands.

If you are able to perform the Figure Eight Movement of the center of gravity without any great difficulties, you can move on to the next stage, which consists of combining the two figure eight movements. They can be combined in a way that fits each within the other, creating a synergy that is unprecedented in its effectiveness. To practice these moves, an average slope offering curves of an average radius is ideal.

The Bearing of the Head and Spinal Column

I began to understand the importance of the spinal axis to skiing during a weekend I spent learning about the Alexander Technique, a method for learning postural efficiency that is especially well known in the theater and classical music worlds. Today an increasing number of athletes are beginning to grasp the benefits offered by this method.

As a kind of welcoming game, the teacher had hung a beam in the garden, which was suspended on either end by a rope. This rope holding the beam in the air was tied to two stakes some thirty centimeters apart from each other and stuck vertically in the ground. Each of these stakes was about fifty centimeters long. Thus the beam was suspended between these four points twenty centimeters above the ground, with enough play to be moved forward of backward and to sway from left to right, if one wished to move it.

The teacher climbed onto the beam, placing one foot behind the other in a line, as if on a tightrope. The beam remained motionless. To climb up on this beam seemed like child's play,

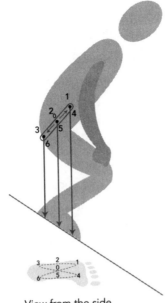

View from the side

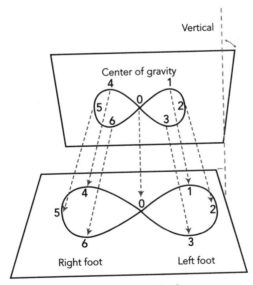

View from the front

*The Double Figure Eight Movement combines the
Figure Eight Movement of the center of gravity and the
Figure Eight Movement of the feet.*

especially using the skwaller stance with which I was quite familiar. But the reality was completely different. One after the other
each of us attending the workshop tried to mount the beam.
The beam would start swaying in every direction as soon as we
put a little weight on it. With a slight impetus I was able to get
up on the beam, which was shaking nonstop in both directions.
What a struggle to remain standing! I could hardly believe my
eyes—or my muscles, for that matter.

The teacher wore a big smile, confident in the effect his
experiment would have. He explained to us that the beam shook
because of poor use of our backs and our spinal columns.

During the two days of the workshop we stretched out on
the ground to learn how to align our back with the nape of our
neck. The work on the ground was broken up by sessions on
good utilization of the hip and knee joints when walking and
climbing hills. When I faithfully followed the instructions concerning the head, the back, the hips, and the knees, my walks
became easier. My weight seemed to evaporate. Sensations were
sublime.

At the end of the weekend we returned to the beam; to
my surprise, when following the instructions, I mounted the
beam and it remained motionless. My positioning was correct,
although a bit timorous. At this moment I realized that the effect
would be the same in snow with one's feet on skis, a snowboard,
or a skwal.

With respect to the head and back, the instructions for maintaining good balance are identical to those taught in chi kung.
Strangely enough, to my knowledge no one has ever examined the
importance of the spinal column and head positioning to gliding
sports. Throughout my research I had concentrated on the placement of the center of my body mass over the ground, without
taking into consideration the role played by the spinal column.

Each of us has a tendency to tilt our heads toward the back, which creates compression at the nape of the neck and contracts the muscles of the neck and shoulders. The simple fact of relaxing the neck muscles encourages the head to resume its natural position on the balance point at the top of the spinal column. When this happens, the head is free and the spinal column resumes its functional effectiveness. The vertical alignment of the centers of the head, the chest, and the belly that ensues as a result improves the perception of the feet on the ground and their rootedness. The perception of the body becomes more refined. The emotions that are closely connected to tension disappear. The mind becomes clear and silent, and consequently more open to the environment. The awareness of space (fore/aft, right/left, high/low) takes on all its meaning. The chains of tension have fallen off.

Here is a very simple exercise that will help you to better grasp the gist of what I am saying.

Sit in a chair and observe what is happening in the area of the neck. For most people the head falls back, the nape of the neck contracts, and this affects the spinal column, which causes various physical compressions: compressed lungs, contracted organs, and so on.

Now start over again, this time concentrating on keeping the neck muscles elongated but relaxed. Your overall perception of your body has probably already changed.

The tipping movement of the head toward the back is strongly emphasized when one sits down. You can observe similar phenomena in a person who is expressing himself verbally, or lifting a heavy package. Seeking to modify the placement of the head only creates tension. Concentrate instead on relaxing the muscles of your neck. The head will find its proper position on its own and the rest of the body will follow.

There are a great number of exercises in the repertoire of the Alexander Technique that you might want to explore for finding balanced posture.

The Way We See

Most of the time, we are selectively reading our environment, which ensures that our eyes only see isolated points on the slope: a mogul or a trail, for example. Our gaze leaps from point to point, remaining still for a short moment on this point here, then jumping to that point over there. There is not a single stable and reliable visual support. Ocular tension grows and spreads into the neck and then into the rest of the body. Projecting toward the obstacle or the information to come, the glider gradually loses contact with the positioning of his body in the moment and becomes nothing more than a mass of tension, buttressed toward the "after."

With this selective vision, large amounts of information escape us. The energy transported by the gaze is projected toward the subject of our tensions in an unconscious manner. We allow our gaze to play a miniscule role in maintaining our physical balance when really it can help us quite a lot.

Observing oneself in action is the first step toward change. In the beginning, all is confusion. This is due to the fact that we only know this selective way of looking at things. There is another way of looking at things, though: it is the gaze centered in the self.

We can observe an entire situation without selecting specific points. When the gaze is centered behind the eyes, the observation of the slope becomes all encompassing and the mind opens to everything that goes into forming the situation. The information comes in on its own, with all its details, and we receive that information serenely and in a relaxed state of mind.

Generally speaking, a person's gaze is fixed on the important object. In the case of skiing, the glider completely projects himself into the supervision of that object. With this new way of looking at things, the object comes to the skier. The energy of looking, which was dispersed before, remains available in the body and at the disposition of the body as it is needed.

Physical availability is born from one's presence in the moment. The heart of the moment is located within oneself. Projection into what is happening or could happen creates tensions, with an inevitable erroneous, and thus useless, vision.

An overall view, using a centered gaze, encourages better comprehension of the situation and better positioning of the body in space. Information cannot reach us instantaneously unless we are visually receptive. Far too often we are anticipating. We are convinced that projection into the beyond, into the next moment, is the appropriate attitude, and that by projecting this way the information will arrive more quickly. But that is not how it is!

Is it possible to maintain an overall view of a situation and capture the important details—false trails, patchy snow—at the same time?

We have a tendency to focus on negative points and difficulties at the expense of the fluidity of the whole. The gaze, like the glide, can be fluid. To achieve this, the gaze should seek support behind the eyes and remain anchored there no matter what is received. This manner of looking at things takes obstacles into account without giving them undue importance. This centered gaze frees the consciousness of an arc of tension toward an object and helps the skier to feel her body and the information it receives for the purpose of experiencing balance within the activity.

In a visual movement that had, until this time, been directed outside, the skier performs a movement toward the interior. This is the great turn around! Thanks to a new way of seeing, the skier (or snowboarder or other glider) preserves his energy and joins his body, his mind, and the surrounding environment yet a little closer.

In studying the illustrations below, if we depict the focusing of energy with a point and the movement of capturing information with an arrow, we have in the first case an arrow that leads the glider toward a point that is confused with the source of information. In the second case, an arrow that comes toward the glider from the object centers the point inside the body.

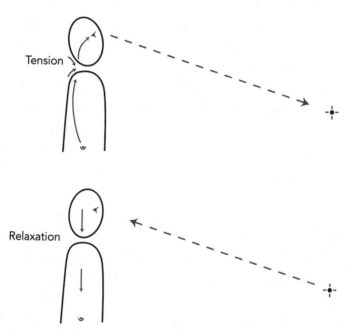

Positioning the head on the spine allows the gaze to move behind the eyes and for objects in the visual field to come to the gaze, rather than the eyes searching for them. This allows for relaxation through the neck and the proper positioning of the head on the spine.

Breath

Respiration is an important element in any sports activity. In skiing and other gliding sports it is important because it carries the oxygen, by way of the bloodstream, that the muscles require to perform an activity. Any physical activity requires a large intake of oxygen. Deep, natural breathing is the ideal. Pressure on the snow when turning and the desire to control it have a tendency to prompt respiratory blockages in the skier, which brings about a loss of muscle availability from which, in turn, his performance will suffer. It is a question of allowing the natural breathing rhythm to establish itself in correspondence with the activity. The body knows what it needs. Breathing movement synchronizes with the movement of the body: when the body compresses, you exhale; you breathe in when the body extends.

There is a correspondence between inhalation and extension, opening up, the push upward and ahead, the separation of the feet, and the movement of the feet toward the back. The corresponding physical phenomena with exhalation are lowering and closing up, moving backward, and the movement of the feet toward the front. Natural breathing can be easily established with practice. All it takes is a thought to remind yourself not to obstruct it.

In order to encourage productive breathing, it is good to feel the complementary relationship between the upper and lower halves of the body. The upper part of the body, including the head, shoulders, arms, and chest, should be loose and available. The legs and pelvis should be heavy and bracing, so as to be solidly connected to the Earth and to oppose the force of gravity. The general rule is that the heavy goes beneath the light. A beginner will place the light beneath the heavy and this reversal will lie in wait to sabotage him. Rigid from the top down because of fear of losing control, he loses his sense of being rooted to the Earth and his supports on the surface will become flimsy and unstable.

Deep, Centered Breathing

A centered movement is a movement that comes to life on the level of the center of gravity, which is to say in the belly. The alignment of the head and chest to the gravity center will introduce a sense of lightness and availability, and consequently effectiveness. An overly willful mind or a haunting emotion can pull the head or chest out of this alignment. This will create tensions and pull the three centers of the head, chest, and belly out of sync.

Respiration plays a major role in achieving centered movement. On the psychological plane, deep breathing imparts peace of mind. On the emotional plane it provides a favorable environment for detachment from external stimuli. On the physical plane, because it reaches the belly, deep breathing transports the energy of the breath into the body's center, then out along the limbs. This breath energy creates a connection between the upper and lower halves of the body. It is the means by which the body becomes conscious. Body and mind reunited can now work as one.

Everything that obstructs us has a tendency to cut the body in two, thus separating the head from the body. "I do not want to be here! Not like this! Something different!" In response the body becomes taut because the mind is pulling it somewhere else. Whatever the present situation may be, it is better if the body and mind join together. Breath restores calm to the mind and to the emotions and directs the energy of thought to the interior of the body for the purpose of the sole thing that matters in the here and now, the conscious gesture adapted to the moment.

Deep breathing is simple and can be practiced when lying down, sitting, standing, or moving. When doing this in the prone position, in a state of doing nothing (to which some of you may not be accustomed), you should observe yourself becoming relaxed and letting go, observe your thoughts, your breath. Do not try and force anything. Observe how a sense of peace will gradually become established. Place your awareness in your belly and feel how the breath enters it and then leaves again.

On some days the exercise can take twenty minutes, others merely two minutes before tensions begin to make their reappearance, or you once again experience the desire to start taking control. You should not try to force the pleasure of doing nothing as you observe your natural breathing. The moment you start exerting your will to achieve this, a shift will take place, causing the energy to disperse and tensions to reappear.

When we do this practice while moving it lets us realize how often we hold our breath in order to stand fast, to hold our ground. Just let it go. Let yourself breathe naturally. The air passage must be free, just like it would be if you were a singer. Verticality and breath should be as one. The diaphragm is flexible and the chest visibly shrinks in size, but inside it is experienced entirely differently. The pulmonary alveoli are no longer straining in search of air; the air is coming to them. This could be described as a kind of self-surrender to natural breathing.

Centered breathing is exhibited by a swelling of the belly that summons air into the lungs.

There are a large number of exercises, books, and courses

(such as yoga) on breathing. Consequently I will not extend myself any further on this subject. If you are able to use deep breathing in your movement, you will be in a position to assess for yourself the benefits it provides and to see for yourself the increased fluidity it can give to you.

CHAPTER 6

From Combat to Harmony

We have now examined how to put ourselves in tune with the natural surroundings, as well as how to get in tune with our bodies. We have also seen how to connect to the environment and how to interpret and employ the physical laws that govern the material world. We still have to investigate the psychological and emotional dimensions of centering, for without this there is no action.

Most of us have a relationship to the outside world based on conflict, the power struggle. It is quite tiring. One must always be on the alert. Could there be another way of doing things?

That is exactly what we are going to learn in this chapter.

To Move Toward . . . or Distance Yourself From

Because of our characters and personal histories, each of us has a tendency to either move toward people, things, novelty or to move away from them.

None of us are all one or the other; we are one or the other depending on the context. For example, I am shy and have a tendency to distance myself from people by refusing to make contact; on the other hand, when I love an activity I go toward it without any doubt or hesitation. We can watch ourselves and

determine if we are more "moving toward" or "going away from" kinds of people. This is all it takes to face a new situation. Once the pattern has been recognized, we can begin to craft a method of working on ourselves to break our habitual patterns.

Physically speaking, a person who "goes toward" will have the tendency to favor skiing on the balls of his feet, whereas someone who "moves away from" will have a tendency to rely more on his heels. The first stage is the realization of this fact, the second is to recognize it in yourself and accept it in the action, and the third is to begin to reorient your body. This practice consists of experiencing the two extreme positions, and provoking and feeling the state of mind associated with each. It is not a question of one being a "good" attitude and the other being "bad"; they are two attitudes that inspire physical and psychological tensions.

To get out of this chain of interlinked tensions, we start by discovering how to establish a sense of being rooted in the Earth. This rooted sensation consists of resting on your feet in a standing position and feeling the ground and the contact of the soles of your feet with the ground. If the mass of your body is projected over the middle of your feet, your body can naturally relax and be freely available for whatever is required of it. This stance permits you to detach yourself from achieving the goal ("moving toward") or fleeing ("moving away from") through orienting your energy toward the center of the body and, more specifically, in that part of the body that connects the body to the Earth: the soles of the feet. This orientation helps us to break free of the automatic response of either moving toward or distancing ourselves from an objective.

But be warned. This impulse will come back at a gallop. When the impulse arises to psychologically extend yourself toward a particular objective, the old habits will reemerge and restore the chains of tensions to their original place. What can you do to avoid this? Once you have planted your "root" it needs to be fed—in other words, this bond to the Earth needs to be recalled and practiced on a regular basis. Snow-gliding sports are in no way an obstacle to this, for, in contrast to walking, the gliding motion is dependent upon a quasi-permanent contact between the middle of the feet and the Earth.

Between "going toward" and "moving away from" there is another state of being; it is a relaxed presence that is ever ready to act. This strong connection to the Earth places us in a new dynamic. Physically relaxed, the mind can open itself to any situation with discernment. There is no room for doubt, which is intimately connected with the projection into what lies ahead, behind, or somewhere else. Projection is the source of doubt; this stimulus arising from the depths of the being lifts the diaphragm and the lungs. When you are in doubt, you will find yourself suspended and cut off from your root, like the inexperienced swimmer who tries to keep his mouth out of the water.

The sensation of being rooted makes it possible to place the body spheres correctly and, primarily, to release tensions. This physical posture frees the mind. Establishing a sense of being rooted to the Earth is essential to centering in the moment.

In each one of us there is a space, a strong point for each of our thoughts and actions, an "empty source." The connection to this source is found in silence and through a movement within. I forget the outside so that I may finally be better present to experience it. The more I "inhabit" my body, the more lucid I am in the world. The energy used by the brain is located within the body. If my mind acts like a tyrant over my body, the body becomes taut in order to reach its goal, and no longer provides either a good supply of energy or the perceptual acuity required for the activity. Stress that usurps control of the body is nothing more than a chain of tensions.

Getting Carried Away by a Situation

The skier desires what is outside of him. Projected toward the goal, he creates a state of general tension in his body: the feet are buttressed, the legs taut, the belly lifts and retracts, the shoulders hunch, the center of gravity is "nailed down." The body is no longer freely available. I am, of course, describing extreme situations, but we can read phenomena of this type in our posture, no matter what the level of our technical ability is. All these tensions are the result of the skier's refusal to accept the situation for what it is. Either he fears or wants, but the essential fact is that he desires the situation to be something other than what it is. These relationships of attraction or repulsion to the surrounding environment characterize the person who seeks to dominate the outside world and who, by the same token, finds himself dominated by it. This is the link of cause and effect.

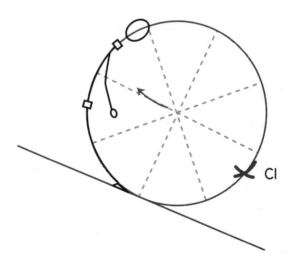

The skier focused outside of himself has a difficult time reaching his goal (denoted by CI: center of interest).

When the skier is outside of himself, he is investing every-thing in the goal instead of in his body and senses, which will lead to the goal. The body is relegated to the function of satel-lite, revolving outside the center of the action. Psychologically carried away by the goal, the skier loses all lucid grasp of the present moment and its requirements. For example, some skiers confuse visual anticipation and physical anticipation. That is to say, they physically stretch toward the end of the turn by replac-ing the curved trajectory of the center of gravity with a straight line that will take them more directly to their objective, the effect of which is for the edge to lose its grip. Often this phenomenon is present but is hard for the skier who is unaware of its exis-tence to detect. Moreover, a good number of joint traumas arise out of this gap between body and mind within an action. One could call that impatience, if not greed.

When we close ourselves off to or refuse to accept the world as it is, we regard the world that surrounds us as an aggres-sor seeking to prevent us from reaching a longed-for objective. Wishing and being able to realize them do not always form a happy couple.

Being at the Heart of the Action

Opening to the outside world begins with accepting the world as it is (to say yes to the world, to say yes to the situation). Open-ness to the world is a state that is simultaneously psychological, emotional, and physical. Internally this openness is constant. It is with this attitude as a starting point that oneness can manifest. Accepting the world for what it is, the skier can create a dynamic equilibrium between his body and the laws governing the world around him. This balance will open the gates of expression for the skier: the gesture adapted to the situation.

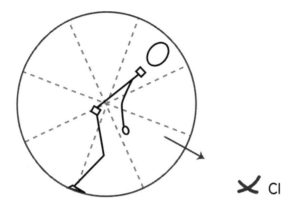

*The centered skier finds himself at the heart of the action and
better able to navigate the outside world.*

For the first step, I center myself and place myself psychologically at the heart of my sensations, at the center of my body. For the next step, I open myself to the information the outside world is sending me while maintaining my anchoring within my body.

The acceptance of being unattached to the goal facilitates this centering and provides the looseness and relaxation necessary for right action. Harmony cannot manifest itself if there is a desire to own the next moment. Harmony finds its source in the "here and now." Responding with acceptance to the myriad situations that follow on each other's heels, the skier makes himself one with the present moment. He enters into the space of expression.

Inner harmony is the source, the strong point for healthy communication with the surrounding environment. Internal conflict drags the skier into a dualistic relationship with the outside world. Inner harmony is founded upon self-acceptance. Not the image one has of oneself or seeks to portray to others, but the being who is uphill of the image, with its qualities and defects, strengths and weaknesses. When the skier truly accepts who he is, the race to possessing everything stops. Tensions fall away. Following this moment, the skier begins to be creative, to express himself freely without having to respond to a more or less conscious diagram.

The simple fact of ceaselessly wishing to be a little farther than the place one is produces a terrible frustration, which is a source of stress and states of limitation. Ceasing to race after what is does not mean simply doing nothing. Quite the contrary! Letting go of what surrounds one awakens peace of mind and self-esteem. What better way could there be to place yourself in the heart of the action?

A movement that originates in the center of gravity permits the skier to communicate effectively with the surrounding environment through the intermediary of his senses: through his feet he perceives the ground, through his hands the air, through his eyes the environment, and so forth.

All of this information is managed to keep the center of the gravity at the center of the movement at every moment. The body has the possibility to open itself to the world if it is inhabited at every moment by a skier who is attuned to that.

Acceptance and Detachment

When I accept being unattached to a goal I have chosen to achieve, I can begin to work to realize my objectives without creating tensions. Separated from the goal, I am consciously living the moment. The goal loses its grip and all that remains are the means I put into the action here and now to reach it and the manner in which I experience these means.

Even if this appears paradoxical, it is through psychological detachment from the goal to be attained that we are able to experience and achieve our aspirations without the normally accompanying tensions.

The acceptance of what is in the present moment and detachment from the goal of the action allow the skier to make the transition from the world of having to the world of being. From the quest for a result, I am reorienting my mind toward the simple fact of being a skier who becomes the act of skiing—a glider who becomes one with the glide. It really is a matter of dying to yourself, in the sense of no longer desiring what comes later but living fully in the "here and now." The world of having is the world of duality, the battle between what I have and what I would like to have, between what I am and what I would like to be. The world of being is the world of the present instant, of the action as well as the realization of the objective but always with the support of the "here and now" and the posture shifting to correspond to every instant. Every moment is a goal in itself, and the sum total of all these interwoven moments forms an action. The appropriate response given to each moment will produce a harmonious realization, whereas if the objective is all that matters, the internal tension and rift that this will create throughout the journey to this goal will ensure that it will not give happiness, even if the goal is achieved.

But just what is that thing we are calling the objective to be attained? In reality it is not a single step but rather several. When it comes to downhill skiing, the goal can simply be arriving at the foot of the mountain without mishap, with the maximum pleasure, or even with a variety of strong sensations, when it is not simply for the pleasure of going fast, impressing the spectators, making progress with a longer term objective in mind, to give someone else pleasure, and so forth. Some objectives really need to be redefined because they are capable of harming and preventing any personal development.

People are not always conscious of their goals. The objective to be obtained can be one of the immediate future: the next curve, the break of the slope. Objectives can be multiple and placed at varying distances in time. Actions have nothing to do with objectives. The sole thing that matters to achieving our objective is our availability to the present moment and to the elements of which this moment is built. Accepting the detachment of the objective from our current situation encourages physical and psychological relaxation for the skier.

Attention and Presence

The dictionary definition of *attention,* in the context that I am presenting, is to fix one's mind on something.

Attention is a movement to the periphery of our being. By concentrating my attention on something, I take possession of it psychologically. In this state of concentrated attention, I am no longer free and available: this kind of concentration eliminates, pushes away, and selects. My body becomes tighter, I project myself out of myself, extend my entire being toward the object of my attention and am pulled into a cause-and-effect mechanism. Projection toward the outside produces internal tension.

Being *present* means first of all being attuned to oneself, inhabiting one's body consciously, being here and now, in an interior silence. This attitude encourages physical relaxation.

I accept everything that has gone into the creation of a situation without repressing any element of it. Centered within myself, I am open to all the things that form the situation, in a relaxed and available manner. Presence within encourages the loosening of internal tensions. Aware of myself, aware of the situation I am in, I am able to act with detachment and spontaneity. The adaptive gesture can be performed because it is no longer an act of lust but a gift to the situation, without any expectation of getting something in return.

Paradoxically, being more present within yourself does not make you a greater egotist but actually produces the complete opposite.

When I am "paying attention"—fixing my mind on some objective—I am stretched out of myself toward the subject that interests (or frightens) me. In a state of presence, I am relaxed and freely available, present to myself, open and receptive to the outside world. In the first situation I am fighting, I am in a dualistic state, I am experiencing the tension caused by I like it/I do not like it; in the second I am relaxed, one with the situation, without making any judgment about who or what is good or bad.

Complementary and Contrary

The body functions like a pump that empties and fills, that raises and lowers, and that shifts from one side to the other. The movements repeat and become dynamic. The body expresses itself through the cyclical use of opposites: fore/aft, up/down, left/right. The opposites are neither fighting each other nor are they freezing into a fixed form. Harmoniously balancing the opposing forces opens the body and its expression in all its dimension.

A complementary nature is not the dualistic opposition of contrary forces. The relation between polar opposites is established in a dynamic manner, which by the same token creates a nondualistic unity. For example, day is opposed to night but when dawn or twilight arrives, the transition from one opposite to the other is carried out quite gently. A complementary nature is not perfect symmetry. Total symmetry is a static structure that smothers all development. In symmetry, all rights to difference vanish. A complementary nature is neither duality nor is it symmetry. It is the perfect middle between opposition (which is destructive) and symmetry (which is static). A complementary nature is based on opposites and creates a third state by the dynamic balancing of opposing forces. This third state, which is displayed through this balance, is the source of all evolution.

A State without an Opposite

Often, most of us find ourselves lost in internal conflict over a situation, a decision that needs to be made: Will I go or will I stay? The opposites that dwell within us are there to help us weigh the pros and cons of every situation that we experience, not for preventing us from taking action. This conflict can be surpassed. The opposites are complementary and the disturbance caused by opposing forces can be transformed if we accept the situation as a whole, and for what it is, not what we would like it to be.

I will provide an example here to help illustrate this point. I have intentionally chosen an example that will trigger a strong emotional response in most people. Similar situations can be found in skiing or snowboarding, with a little less at stake perhaps unless we are talking about extreme skiing.

I am climbing up a rock face alone, without a rope. I find myself in difficulty quite a few feet above the ground. If I fall, I will get hurt. I am having trouble turning back or proceeding upward. My thoughts focus on the problems that a fall will cause and my desire not to live through all that (to fall/not to fall).

If I remain stationed in this state of mind, all my energy will go toward seeking to resolve the problem intellectually. I am stretched taut, my mind is racing back and forth, my hand is

becoming strained, my muscles are stiffening, and so forth. The conflict has become well established and nothing is happening. At this moment I do not have much time left and I have to direct myself toward the sole thing that is good for me: manufacturing an exit and gathering all my energy together for the sole purpose of pursuing my development.

To fall or not to fall is another way of saying to die or not to die. But this is not living. There is another state between these two opposites, between blocking everything totally or letting go of everything—that is the source point. Balance can only be experienced when in a relaxed state. The return of peace to the mind grants fluidity to movement.

"There where your thought resides is where your energy resides," the martial arts masters say. The reorientation of the mind outside of the duality imposed by the situation, while still taking it into consideration, opens the door to nonduality, to the image of the axis of the balancing pole with the plates of the scales. The immutable balance is in the axis. If I identify with one of the plates of the scales, the other goes up. Nor is removing the plates to identify with the axis possible, because the axis by itself is nothing. One cannot be an axis without a satellite, without the plates of the scales.

In the preceding example, the scale plates are the rock face and the void. As long as things are going well, I have no reason to ask myself whether I am the balancing pole or the plates of the scales, but once a problem surfaces, I identify with the rock face and deny the void. I become physically one with the rock and my mind focuses on the void. I am cut in two. In reality, I am neither the rock face nor the void, but I take both into account. If with my body I look for the right distance, the balance point between the rock face and the void, the point of the least effort that corresponds to the perfect placement, my body will remain available longer in the search for the solution to the problem. The movement leads to the exit.

Letting Go

Nothing is fixed. Everything moves, more or less quickly, from the largest body of matter to the most refined, from the smallest particle to the entire universe.

Too often, man seeks to fix things to a set order (it is reassuring), and this attitude is reflected in the movements of his body. On the snow, a gliding engine beneath his feet, a person passes from the solid Earth to a slippery milieu that offers little comfort. Immediately he seeks to recover that lost stability. The backward-leaning stance indicates a desire to recover the state of nonsliding. He does not wish to let go. This comportment concerns the veteran skier as well as the beginner.

The stomach knotted, shoulders hunched up, the shoulder blades pressed together, the toes curled under, supporting the body on the heels: all these physical attitudes indicate to an observer as well as the skier (if he is attuned to his body and hears what it is telling him) a feeling of fear, a denial of the present, a restraint in the action, a desire to extract oneself out of this situation, and the fact of not taking on a presence in the world. This does not merely concern an attitude adopted when faced with a particularly complex situation; it is a way of approaching life. The body has recorded all these fears and anxieties since the moment of conception and they manifest at every moment. All these knots are like psychological and emotional crutches. We think we are protecting ourselves. What nonsense! If we wish to swim, we have to let go of the side of the pool, not to mention push ourselves toward the other side with the entire body stretched toward that goal.

Swimming is relaxation in its pure state. But no relaxation is possible for the beginner unless it is realized that the distance to the other side needs to be adapted to his or her abilities.

To really grasp the nature of relaxation in skiing or the other snow gliding sports, a very gentle slope with a natural stopping point is chosen in order to avoid any tension associated with the situation. Beginning from this sensation of well-being, we observe an inner state of potential openness to what surrounds us and, by the same token, the possibility of letting go of the before and after. Letting go is simply to start skiing with no other purpose than to be there at that precise moment, to leave the home port and observe the great ballet of the physical laws that apply to our bodies and to the snow and that produce this incredible phenomenon known as skiing. Letting go can very easily be experienced when coming to a stop because it involves a psychological itinerary, an internal attitude toward something that is outside of us but is of capital importance with respect to our survival. Clinging to life prevents us from acting freely. The fear of losing what we have prevents us from living and expressing ourselves.

Letting go is an internal state that displays itself in deeds and gestures. It sits between high tension and complete relaxation, between "going toward" and "moving away from." This state helps us to emerge from a mode of reactive expression and change our course toward an active mode. The action originates in the heart.

Hiking up a mountain stream by jumping from rock to rock is a good way to get a sense of the phenomenon. In the beginning the stone you are jumping *to* is important, then gradually the stone you are jumping *from* takes on greater importance. One lingers there as long as possible. One approaches it the better to move far away from it, the better to leap. Little by little we become more present inside our feet; the body gains importance and becomes the key piece in the game of movement. The grip upon the stone grows blurry and begins to be experienced as a component of movement. It is a note, but it is surely not the score and most definitely not the musician. The importance that one gives to it is completely relative. The fluidity of the movement at the center of gravity becomes the heart of the individual's concerns.

How many skiers are convinced that they will be guaranteed greater control by displaying a violent push for support at each turn? As in the beginning of the exercise concerning the stones, the more that all that exists is the source of support, the more fluidity is missing from one's movements. Movement is composed of a multitude of successive and interpenetrating moments. Fluidity is born from the consideration we give to each one of these moments.

Letting go assists us in breaking free from our constricting anchorages so that we can finally be completely available to the situation as a whole.

Spontaneity

To make one's own world coincide with the surrounding world requires ceaseless labor on the self. Forgetting her objective for a moment, making room for the requirements of the environment and no longer fearing or desiring, makes it possible for the skier to perform an action that emanates from her, with no other purpose but to perform it. Physical expression (which is not mental expression) is conditioned by universal physical laws. The body submitting consciously to these laws will liberate itself. The ego will free itself. The action becomes the conscious expression of the laws of nature.

The world of the skier coinciding with the outside world: this is spontaneity.

The skier no longer views himself as a separate entity from the world but physically experiences the interdependence existing between human and nature. Complying with its laws, accepting them, and compromising with them allows the human being to surpass the limits of his or her petty ego to consciously experience the great ballet of universal laws.

An ego that is greedy for results will not be able to hear what the body is saying. The body sends out warnings by means of tension, and the ego continues to drag that body to the goal it longs for. Being attuned to the body allows one to go beyond this state of limitation. The body is no longer considered as something that hinders an action from being accomplished but as a vehicle for awareness and realization.

Emotional Centering

The Merriam-Webster definition of *emotion* is as follows: "a conscious mental reaction (as anger or fear) subjectively experienced as strong feeling usually directed toward a specific object and typically accompanied by physiological and behavioral changes in the body." By extension it would be a sensation (agreeable or disagreeable) that is considered from an emotional perspective.

Emotion is physically related to the region of the chest—the area of the heart, lungs, breath, and diaphragm. An external stimulus—the unexpected presence of an object in your path, for example—produces a positive or negative effect upon the individual. It prompts a tension, often associated with a constricted in-breath, that brings about a sense of ill ease connected with the negative assessment of the situation, as well as the loss of a measure of objectivity and one's strong rooted connection to the ground. Stimulus has a power over the individual. But who grants this power to the stimulus if not the individual himself? It involves a question of power and possession. We project our fears and desires over events, which creates a gap between ourselves and reality. The emotional person is always saying: "me, me, me!" internally. A person who tries to possess something will find himself possessed by the object of his desire. It is like the boomerang effect. If I allow myself to be carried away by a situation, emotion appears. I no longer exist. There is only the object, the emotion, and the tension that the emotion engenders. Emotion is not a means for knowledge. When information from the outside world comes to us through the filter of our emotions, it arrives deformed and demanding an adaptive response, a response of a reactive nature.

Let's look at an example. A skier is hurtling down a slope at high speed. He suddenly spots a large break in the slope. On discovering this gap, the skier, who had until then been balanced over his skis, stands up, and performs a slight movement in retreat, combined with a deep inhalation. The three synchronized actions uproot the skier, who can no longer provide an adaptive response. Here is another example: the skier arrives at the site of a competition she has entered and finds that the conditions are perfect for her—the snow is good, the challenge of the trail is perfect, the person she most wants to be there has arrived. The skier, emotionally moved by this situation, gets excited. The emotion is significant, and although positive, uproots her and causes her to lose some of her lucidity.

An emotion experienced as either repulsive or attractive still remains an emotion, and therefore invites a state of limitation. It produces a heightened and destabilizing inhalation. It creates tension, a gap between the event and the adaptive action. It does not allow for effective management of a situation. Quite to the contrary. It carries us away. We breathe it in and it carries us off.

Seeking to dominate the emotion is a form of repression inflicted on the body. We should accept the emotion and experience it fully so as to understand its function in the body. Once the emotion has been experienced without any denial or attempt to reject it, it loses its power. The closer we go back to its root, to the conditions of its appearance, the greater our understanding of it will be, and we will gradually identify with the emotion less and less before finally eradicating it completely.

Emotion is connected to poor control of one's breathing. Learning how to breathe correctly permits us to discover emotional centering, and the monitoring and orientation of our thoughts toward what is essential for any given moment.

I consider emotional centering as a state of being, a state of acceptance of what is, a radiant and positive availability directed toward all the things that make up the various situations we experience.

Contrary to emotion, the initiative for emotional centering comes from within, it comes from the individual and addresses all components of the situation. There is no longer any question of dividing phenomena into good or bad; rather, we accept the things that appear in our lives for what they are. With this positive attitude as its starting point, any action will take on its full dimension. This state of being allows one to act in a kind of lucid oneness, and no longer simply in reaction to a stimulus. It is being open and present to what is. Facing the world (of which the body is a part) and the laws that govern it, the skier can achieve the perfect gesture for the situation. He can move beyond his fears and desires. I am both witness and actor in the world of manifestation. I love the world that surrounds me and I express myself in its heart. When situations change and become difficult, I maintain this attitude and quality of being. It is the perfect attitude. I remain one with the situation. My actions and my responses to situations are more measured and adaptive. They are connected to my perception of the world. I communicate with the world I observe through the intermediary of my body (and in respect of it), and always listen to my body as a friend and extension of myself.

Rather than seeking to pull myself psychologically out of a difficult spot, I accept the situation and become one with it.

There is a notion of harmony and respect for the world in this approach. The skier perceives her body and the surrounding environment, and acts through them. The skier's body and the surrounding environment have become as one. The skier views both with detachment and a sense of presence simultaneously; she does not try to master them but to let them exist as a single entity.

To become one with the situation is the source of right action, equilibrium, centering, and ease in movement. This, in a word, is harmony. A conscious link is established between two centers: the center of the Earth and the center of the body. At this moment the skier experiences a dual sensation: being both the spectator and actor of his body. By virtue of this freedom provided by the mind, the body loosens up and is charged with positive energies and refined perceptions. The body is no longer simply a trigger in the grip of a hand that would be the mind. It finds its true dimension anew. By no longer imposing his mind on his body, the skier is no longer a tyrant but an accomplice who listens, gives, and receives.

The notion of effort has no place in this relationship to the body. When the skier adopts this attitude for the first time, she may feel that she has not "given her all" because she did not

mobilize every possible scrap of energy in her performance. Nonsense! The performance integrates energy savings. The skier is potentially a supporter of the least effort, but one that is in the interest of achieving the best results.

Summary Chart

Throughout the last chapters we have been examining our habits and seeing their implications on our actions. This chart provides a direct comparison of the two fundamentally different approaches we can take, if we accept the option of taking the path from the world of having to the world of being. Examining the two attitudes, you'll see that these different approaches go far beyond the context of snow sports.

Repression	Expression
Needing to have	Being
A person who is off center or self-centered	A person who is centered within and centered in the world
Withdrawn into the self	Open
1. Off-centered individual	**1.** Centered individual
Unbalanced, attracted by the goal	Balanced, displaying self-mastery
2. Reactive nature	**2.** Complementary nature
Conflict-driven relationship with the environment	Balance between the individual and the environment with which he interacts
Denial of external conditions	Acceptance of everything that makes up a situation

Repression (continued)	Expression (continued)
Separated from the world	Open to the world
By not taking physical laws into consideration, the body suffers or finds itself dragged into a chain of unmanageable causes and effects (permanent imbalance)	Taking all of the component elements of the existing situation into consideration, the person makes objective and impersonal decisions
3. Egoism: bending the world to one's will	**3.** Open to the natural world through the senses
A person who lives in his or her own world	Connected with the world
A person who imposes himself on the world	Attuned to the world
A person who is mentally agitated and cut off from the world	A calm and receptive mind: a person who experiences the world
4. State of mind that invites vulnerability, weakness	**4.** State of mind that protects against assaults
Gap between reality and the idea one has of it	Can withdraw or attack depending on the needs of the moment
Body is taut, subdued	Body is active and relaxed
Strong emotions	Centered emotions
5. Approach that lacks acknowledgment of distinctions	**5.** Approach that acknowledges the uniqueness of each moment
Me: the unique one who imposes his will	The unique passes through the ego
Stereotypical gestures	Adaptive gestures
Movements in reaction, whose origin is imbalance	Respect for the laws that govern movement makes right action possible

Repression (continued)	Expression (continued)
6. Tension: blockages	**6.** Relaxation: new perceptions
Strong sensations	Subtle sensations
Initiative dictated by the outside	Initiative coming from within
Pulled out of one's self in imbalance	Conscious of being centered within an autonomy
Slave: outside influences have full powers	Not dependent on attaining
Gap between the situation and the idea one has of it; loss of lucidity, ill at ease	Attuned to the body and the environment, respect for the unique character of each situation, of each moment
Out of touch	Feeling "in step"
7. Seeking to master and hold firm	**7.** Openness: letting go (which is not the same as letting things drop)
Crystallization	Fluidity in the moment
Frozen attitude, regression	Dynamic attitude, expression
Self-destruction	Creative energy
8. Attachment to the goal	**8.** Detachment from a goal to be attained
Having the upper hand	Being the action
Extended toward the goal	Present in the moment
9. The marionette	**9.** The aware person
Prisoner of him- or herself	The limiting body becomes the attuned body

CHAPTER 7

The Katas of Skiing

Katas are movement sequences that are performed before a presentation; in Japan, where the term originates, *katas* refer to the basic forms that can be found in all martial arts techniques. Some may believe that these movements are merely warm-ups. In reality they go far beyond that. The katas presented in this book have been created with an eye to placing the skier in conscious relation with his body and with the natural environment that surrounds him.

If the skier has worked earlier in the day on other exercises—such as relaxing and centering, for example—the katas will be all the more rapidly effective, as they will then become an extension of this earlier work.

Kata 1: Centering

Centering is the simplest kata, and yet it is the most important one. The purpose of this kata is to facilitate the skier's contact with the Earth by establishing a relationship between the center of the body and the center of the Earth by means of the feet. This basic stance can also be used for coming to a flat stop when sliding to face the slope one has just come down.

1. Find your alignment: head, chest, abdomen.
2. Go into a semicompressed stance: ankles, knees, hips flexed.
3. Hold your head loosely, as if suspended from a string. The nape of the neck is disengaged, your chin is slightly tucked in, and your gaze is directed at the horizon.
4. Calm your mind. Even if thoughts continue to trickle through, maintain your awareness of your body and your stance.
5. Relax the upper half of your body: shoulders, neck, arms, and chest. Your arms should hang down alongside your body a little in front, without touching your chest.
6. Open the centers of your hands to relax your shoulders and arms to encourage the circulation of energy into your hands, and feel the space surrounding you.
7. Relax your abdomen, making it freely available; your pelvis should fall into the proper position, with the lumbar curve reduced.
8. Place your body over your feet. As you center your body's mass equally over the two feet, open the centers of your feet to feel your connection with the Earth.
9. Maximize the muscle compression in the lower half of the body to fight against the pull of gravity.

Kata 2: Fore/Aft Movements

Compress and extend in accordance with the design of the spinal column. This will produce a longitudinal movement of body mass, which pushes the engine into the slope without expending effort used in pivoting and guides the turn without expending effort in rotation.

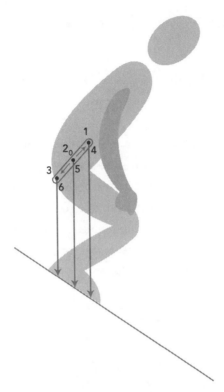

Compress and extend to follow the alignment of the spinal column.

Kata 3: Lateral Movements, or Edging

Ski down a slope and come to a stop. Starting from the center of the feet, gradually move away from your stopping point laterally, first with lateral movements of the whole body, and then with lateral movement of the knees in a flexed position.

Now do the same thing in movement, using the edges of the skis. Feel the axis moving away from the center of gravity, passing through the midfemur, the midtibia, and reaching the center of the foot. Observe the rotation of the head of the femur in its hip socket.

Kata 4: The Figure Eight Movement of the Feet

We have looked at the fore/aft and lateral movements in katas 2 and 3. In this next kata we will use a movement that combines both.

The movement always starts from the center of the foot and returns there. Generally, on skis, a snowboard, or a skwal, the body mass is projected 50/50 over both feet, then as a rule oscillates from 30 to 70 percent from one foot to the other.

The next instructions all reference the art below. 0 is the center of the foot. The / represents the zone subject to the greatest pressure from the weight of the body.

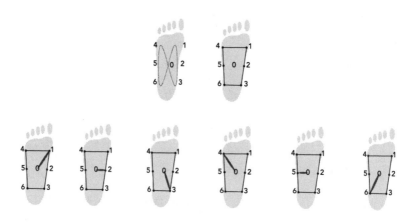

Your feet are parallel and apart at a flat stop. Visualize the movement internally and circulate your awareness following points 0 to 6 on one foot, then the other foot, and then both together.

Now perform the movement by projecting your body weight over those same points, in succession, from 0 to 6. Finally, on a gentle slope in a stance designed for speed, perform the Figure

Eight Movement of the feet with a simple fore/aft motion, using compression and extension of the ankle and laterally shifting the feet by moving the knees laterally. The body mass does not move; it is the feet that move beneath the mass.

Kata 5: The Figure Eight Movement of the Center of Gravity

Standing with feet apart (not on skis), place your index fingers facing each other on your belly, at the level of the center of gravity. Place your awareness at the point of contact of both fingers. Your shoulders should be relaxed (throughout the entire sequence), the neck disengaged, head straight, mind calm, your legs semiflexed, and your abdomen well relaxed over your feet.

Perform a slow run through of the Figure Eight Movement with your hands at the center of gravity. Once you feel familiar with tracing this movement with your hands, move the center of gravity through the Figure Eight Movement at the same time. A wide stance will expand the size of the movement at the center of gravity.

When you can feel the motion inside, stop moving your hands.

On a gentle, wide slope, practice the Figure Eight Movement of the center of gravity as you ski. This movement can be practiced on any snow engine—all it requires is an adaptation of the pelvis as required by the engine.

Kata 6: Synchronizing the Two Figure Eight Movements

This sequence requires mastery of the previous two katas. Choose a shallow slope that will not present you with any difficulties.

Practice the Figure Eight Movement of the feet together with the Figure Eight Movement of the center of gravity. Repeat the movement many times—just be consistent in your turning radius. It is through repetition that you can make the cycle automatic. With more experience, the variations will come of their own accord.

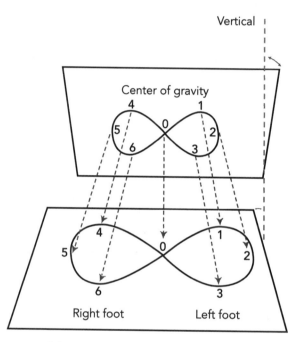

A schematic of the Figure Eight Movement of the center of gravity (top) and the Figure Eight Movement of the feet (bottom) on skis.

Kata 7: The Vertical Play of the Hands

In the stopped stance, go into the position of being rooted: legs semiflexed, pelvis tucked in for a straight back, relaxed shoulders, head weightless as if suspended from a string, chin and shoulders slightly tucked in. Hold your ski poles in front of your feet, allowing the natural separation of the shoulders and letting the armpits completely disengage from any contact with the body. Breathe slowly and deeply to bring sensitivity and peace of mind. Once you have achieved this state, slowly raise your arms to shoulder level until the baskets of the ski poles are even with your hands, with the poles perpendicular to your forearms, if not slightly higher (up to 110 degrees). Your elbows should be semiflexed and your shoulders relaxed. Breathe slowly, without trying to synchronize your breathing with the movement. Keep the arms raised for several seconds before starting to slowly lower them, maintaining awareness of your hands. Your hands should not drop below the elbows.

Repeat this movement several times. Feel what is taking place internally along the spinal column.

In a second phase, the descending movement of your hands can be combined with flexing your lower limbs. Synchronize your breath with this movement. The movement of your ascending hands can be combined with the extension of your lower limbs and also synchronized with deep, slow abdominal breathing.

This sequence encourages the connection between the upper half of the body and the belly, and the connection between the belly and the ground, by way of the center of the feet.

In practice this kata teaches us, when entering a turn, to position the hand that is on the outside of the curve upward (at shoulder level, maximum) and to gradually lower your elbow and hand. Your hand should go no lower than your elbow. Your wrist should be positioned so that the ski pole (held by all five fingers) remains, at a minimum, perpendicular to your forearm, so that it creates an open angle between them. The lowering of the forearm is combined with your exhalation and the lowering of the body through compression. Your hand should not revolve around the spinal column. It should revolve because your entire body is turning.

The physical advantage of this kata is that the perception center of the hand becomes more open, the upper half of the body is free, and the feet become increasingly rooted. The lowering of the elbows combined with the stretching of the wrists encourages the thoracic cage to expand, the shoulders to relax, and tension and suspended emotion to drop, and produces relaxed breathing. By the same token it prevents your body from moving like a bouncing ball.

The hand accompanies the compression and helps regulate the pressure put on the snow. Throughout the turn, the hand remains in the same vertical axis parallel to the spinal column, which enables the skier to maintain the body in alignment with the feet.

Kata 8: Compression/Extension on a Steep Slope

When skiing down a steep slope, or in powder, or over bumps, you will flex your legs in order to maintain contact as you go through the fall line, then extend the legs to maintain contact and complete the turn.

The warm-up exercise is done on a flat surface and consists of visualizing skiing a curve in a compressed stance. You push off on the front foot to enter the turn, then extending upward and behind the middle of the foot for the phase of coming out of the turn.

This kata can be used on a gentle slope in order to make wide traverses. While this exercise is pleasant to do because of the sensations it provides, it is not considered a high-performance movement for competition.

CHAPTER 8

The Katas of Snowboarding

Some of the instructions in this chapter are repeated from the previous chapter on the katas for skiing. Just as they are for skiing, katas for snowboarding are movements or sequences that are rehearsed before a performance. This performance can be a training exercise, a competition, or simply a session of snowboarding. Some may consider these movements as warm-ups, but in reality they go far beyond that. These katas have been designed to place the snowboarder in a relationship of awareness with his body and the natural environment that surrounds him.

If the snowboarder has worked earlier in the day on the relaxing and centering exercises discussed earlier, the katas will be all the more effective as they will then merely be an extension of the earlier practice.

Kata 1: Centering

Centering is the simplest kata, and yet it is the most important one. The purpose of this kata is to facilitate the snowboarder's contact with the Earth by establishing a relationship between the center of the body and the center of the Earth by means of the feet. This basic stance can also be used for coming to a flat stop when sliding to face the slope one has just come down.

1. Find your alignment: head, chest, abdomen.
2. Go into a semicompressed stance: ankles, knees, hips flexed.
3. Hold your head loosely, as if suspended from a string. The nape of the neck is disengaged, your chin is slightly tucked in, and your gaze is directed at the horizon.
4. Calm your mind. Even if thoughts continue to trickle through, maintain your awareness of your body and your stance.
5. Relax the upper half of your body: shoulders, neck, arms, and chest. Your arms should hang down alongside your body a little in front, without touching your chest.
6. Open the centers of your hands to relax your shoulders and arms to encourage the circulation of energy into your hands, and feel the space surrounding you.
7. Relax your abdomen, making it freely available; your pelvis should fall into the proper position, with the lumbar curve reduced.
8. Place your body over your feet. As you center your body's mass equally over the two feet, open the centers of your feet to feel your connection with the earth.
9. Maximize the muscle compression in the lower half of the body to fight against the pull of gravity.

The feet and body are perpendicular to the axis of the snowboard (a position that is determined by the placement of the fastenings). Consequently, once this basic stance has been found, the snowboarder will orient his head, and only his head, toward the tip of the snowboard, while leaving the nape of his neck free and relaxed.

Kata 2: Falling Leaf Movement

Starting from a basic stance balanced on both feet, this kata consists of shifting the body mass from one foot to the other. This alternating sideslip motion mimics the movement of a falling leaf.

In this exercise, the slope should be fairly steep. The board perpendicular to the slope should be flat enough to glide in a sideslip. The front foot should be used to push the tip of the board into the slope without any effort, and without any intentional rotation. This is the basic movement for entering a turn. The center of gravity goes toward the front and down slope. The action is the same for the back foot. It will serve to ensure that the board sideslips to return to a position across the slope. There is no effort expended in rotation.

Once this kata has been performed on the heels, it can also be done on the toes, meaning with your back to the downhill slope.

Kata 3: Lateral Movements, or Edging

Snowboard down a slope and come to a stop. Starting from the center of the feet, gradually move the board away from your stopping point laterally, first with fore/aft movements of the entire body; then pushing from the knees, accompanied by the upper half of the body, to move on to the toes; and finally with elevation of the toes while maintaining a compressed stance combined with a general tilt of your body toward the back, to move on to the heels.

Once you are moving, practice edging. Feel the axis moving away from the center of gravity, passing through the midfemur, the midtibia, and reaching the center of the foot. Then shift the axis toward the toes by using the body movements described in the previous paragraph.

With this kata, avoid flexing the hips to push the head forward or pull the pelvis back.

Kata 4: The Figure Eight Movement of the Feet

In this next kata, we will explore a turning movement that brings both lateral and fore/aft movements into play.

The movement starts at the center of the board and returns to this point. Whether on snowboard, skwal, or skis, the body mass is generally projected 50/50 over both feet, then as a rule oscillates from 30 to 70 percent from one foot to the other.

The flat phase facilitates the orientation of the board with respect to the fall line. The phase on the edge moves the board laterally, away from the fall line. The juxtaposition of the two phenomena in the Figure Eight Movement generates a wide range of trajectories.

Beginning at a flat stop, visualize the Figure Eight Movement internally (without doing it physically). Circulate your awareness following the points 0 to 6 from one foot on to the next. Then perform the Figure Eight Movement by projecting the weight of the body over the feet following points 0 through 6. Use the movements from katas 2 and 3 to avoid making any maladjusted movements.

Now, on a gentle slope and in the basic stance (see kata 1), perform the Figure Eight Movement of the feet with a simple fore/aft workout of the foot through the compression and extension of the shin and the lateral shifting of the feet. The mass of the body should not move; it is the feet that should be moving beneath the mass in a Figure Eight Movement.

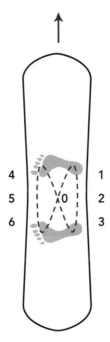

The Figure Eight Movement on a snowboard

Kata 5: The Figure Eight Movement of the Center of Gravity

Try to perform the same Figure Eight Movement around the center of gravity. First when stopped, then in curves down a gentle slope, perform this movement while keeping an average turn radius, without making your turn too tight (keep the board in the slope). Once you have gotten the feeling down of the Figure Eight Movement of the center of gravity, you can then begin to synchronize it with the Figure Eight Movement of the feet.

Kata 6: Synchronizing the Two Figure Eight Movements

This sequence requires mastery of the previous two katas. Choose a shallow slope that will not present you with any difficulties. Practice the Figure Eight Movement of the feet together with the Figure Eight Movement of the center of gravity. Repeat the movement many times—just be consistent in your turning radius. It is through repetition that you can make the cycle automatic. With more experience, the variations will come of their own accord.

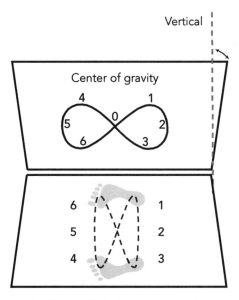

A schematic of the Figure Eight Movement of the center of gravity (top) and the Figure Eight Movement of the feet (bottom) on the snowboard.

Kata 7: Compression/Extension on a Steep Slope

When snowboarding down a steep slope, or in powder, or over bumps, you will flex your legs in order to maintain contact as you go through the fall line, then extend them to complete the turn.

The warm-up exercise is done on a flat surface and consists of visualizing riding a curve in a compressed stance. You push off on the front foot to enter the turn, then extending upward and behind the middle of the foot for the phase of coming out of the turn.

This kata can be used on a gentle slope in order to make wide traverses. While this exercise is pleasant to do because of the sensations it provides, it is not considered a high-performance movement for competition.

CHAPTER 9

The Katas of Skwalling

As with skiing and snowboarding, these katas are movements or sequences that are rehearsed before a performance. This performance can be a training exercise, a competition, or simply a session of skwalling. Some may simply consider these movements as warm-ups. But in reality they go far beyond that. These katas have been designed to place the skwaller in a relationship of awareness with his body and the natural environment that surrounds him.

If the skwaller has worked earlier in the day (say, when getting up in the morning) on the relaxing and centering exercises discussed earlier, the katas will be all the more effective, as they will then merely be an extension of the earlier practice.

Kata 1: Centering

Centering is the simplest kata, and yet it is the most important one. The purpose of this kata is to facilitate the skwaller's contact with the Earth by establishing a relationship between the center of the body and the center of the Earth by means of the feet. This basic stance can also be used for coming to a flat stop when sliding to face the slope one has just come down.

1. Find your alignment: head, chest, abdomen.
2. Go into a semicompressed stance: ankles, knees, hips flexed. The knees are pressed solidly together.
3. Hold your head loosely, as if suspended from a string. The nape of the neck is disengaged, your chin slightly is tucked in, and your gaze is directed at the horizon.
4. Calm your mind. Even if thoughts continue to trickle through, maintain your awareness of your body and your stance.
5. Relax the upper half of your body: shoulders, neck, arms, and chest. Your arms should hang down alongside your body a little in front, without touching your chest.
6. Open the centers of your hands to relax your shoulders and arms to encourage the circulation of energy into your hands, and feel the space surrounding you.
7. Relax your abdomen, making it freely available; your pelvis should fall into the proper position, with the lumbar curve reduced.
8. Place your body over your feet. As you center your body's mass equally over the two feet, open the centers of your feet to feel your connection with the earth.
9. Maximize the muscle compression in the lower half of the body to fight against the pull of gravity.

The feet are placed one in front of the other with good ankle flexing, which facilitates good contact between the centers of the soles of the feet with the Earth. The shoulders and pelvis are perpendicular to the axis of the skwal. A good compression of the hips (more than for skiing) guides the placement and relaxation of the entire body.

Kata 2: Falling Leaf Movement

Starting from a basic stance balanced on both feet, this kata consists of shifting the body mass from one foot to the other. Compression and extension in accord with the design of the spinal column will produce a longitudinal movement of body mass, which pushes the engine into the slope without expending effort in pivoting and guides the turn without expending effort in rotation. This alternating sideslip motion mimics the movement of a falling leaf.

In this exercise, the slope should be fairly steep. The board should be perpendicular to the slope and flat enough to glide in a sideslip. The front foot should be used to push the tip of the board into the slope without any effort, and no intentional rotation. This is the basic movement for entering a turn. The center of gravity goes toward the front and down slope. The action is the same for the back foot. It will serve to ensure that the skwal sideslips to return to a position across the slope. There is still no effort expended in rotation.

Once this kata has been performed in one direction, it can be done in the other direction.

Kata 3: Lateral Movements, or Edging

Glide down a slope and come to a stop. Starting from the center of the feet, gradually move away from your stopping point laterally, first with lateral movements of the entire body; then pushing from the knees, accompanied by the upper half of the body; then, once you are moving, practice edging.

Feel the axis moving away from the center of gravity, passing through the midfemur, the midtibia, and reaching the center of the foot. Then shift the axis toward the toes by using the body movements described above. Avoid pushing the hips laterally and having too much of an open angle between the line of the hips and the axis of the skwal.

Kata 4: The Figure Eight Movement of the Feet

In this next kata we will explore a turning movement that brings both lateral and fore/aft movements into play.

The movement starts at the center of the board and returns to this point. Whether on snowboard, skwal, or skis, the body mass is generally projected 50/50 over both feet, then as a rule oscillates from 30 to 70 percent from one foot to the other.

Beginning at a flat stop, visualize the Figure Eight Movement internally (without doing it physically). Circulate your awareness following the points 0 to 6 on one foot, then on the other,

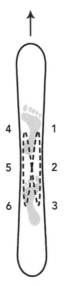

The Figure Eight Movement on a skwal

then both together. Next, perform the Figure Eight Movement by projecting the weight of the body over the feet in sequence from point 0 through point 6. Use the movements from katas 2 and 3 to avoid making any maladjusted movements.

Now, on a gentle slope and in a stance designed for speed, perform the Figure Eight Movement of the feet with a simple fore/aft motion, using compression and extension of the ankle and the lateral shifting of the feet. The mass of the body does not move; it is the feet that move beneath the body.

Kata 5: The Figure Eight Movement of the Center of Gravity

Standing with feet apart (not on the skwal), place your index fingers facing each other on your belly, at the level of the center of gravity. Place your awareness at the point of contact of both fingers. Your shoulders should be relaxed (throughout the entire sequence), the neck disengaged, head straight, mind calm, your legs semiflexed, and your abdomen well relaxed over your feet.

Perform a slow run through of the Figure Eight Movement with your hands at the center of gravity. Once you feel familiar with tracing this movement with your hands, move the center of gravity through the Figure Eight Movement at the same time. A wide stance will expand the size of the movement at the center of gravity.

When you can feel the motion inside, stop moving your hands.

On a gentle, wide slope, practice the Figure Eight Movement of the center of gravity as you skwal. This movement can be practiced on any snow engine—all it requires is an adaptation of the pelvis as required by the engine.

Kata 6: Synchronizing the Two Figure Eight Movements

This sequence requires mastery of the previous two katas. Choose a shallow slope that will not present you with any difficulties. Practice the Figure Eight Movement of the feet together with the Figure Eight Movement of the center of gravity. Repeat the movement many times—just be consistent in your turning radius. It is through repetition that you can make the cycle automatic. With more experience, the variations will come of their own accord.

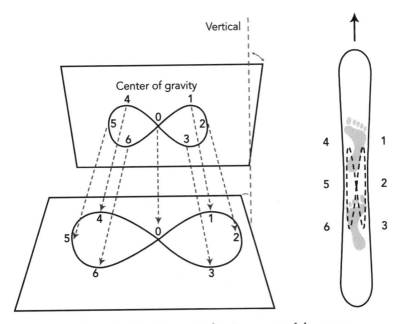

A schematic of the Figure Eight Movement of the center of gravity (top) and the Figure Eight Movement of the feet (bottom) on the skwal.

Kata 7: The Vertical Play of the Hands

In the stopped stance, go into the position of being rooted: legs semiflexed, pelvis tucked in for a straight back, relaxed shoulders, head weightless as if suspended from a string, chin and shoulders slightly tucked in. Hold your poles in front of your feet, allowing the natural separation of the shoulders and letting the armpits completely disengage from any contact with the body. Breathe slowly and deeply to bring sensitivity and peace of mind. Once you have achieved this state, slowly raise your arms to shoulder level until the baskets of the poles are even with your hands, with the poles perpendicular to your forearms, if not slightly higher (up to 110 degrees). Your elbows should be semiflexed and your shoulders relaxed. Breathe slowly, without trying to synchronize your breathing with the movement. Keep the arms raised for several seconds before starting to slowly lower them, maintaining awareness of your hands. Your hands should not drop below the elbows.

Repeat this movement several times. Feel what is taking place internally along the spinal column.

In a second phase, the descending movement of your hands can be combined with flexing your lower limbs. Synchronize your breath with this movement. The movement of your ascending hands can be combined with the extension of your lower limbs and also synchronized with deep, slow abdominal breathing.

This sequence encourages the connection between the upper half of the body and the belly, and the connection between the belly and the ground, by way of the center of the feet.

In practice this kata teaches us, when entering a turn, to position the hand that is on the outside of the curve upward (at shoulder level, maximum) and to gradually lower your elbow and hand. Your hand should go no lower than your elbow. Your wrist should be positioned so that the pole (held by all five fingers) remains, at a minimum, perpendicular to your forearm, so that it creates an open angle between them. The lowering of the forearm is combined with your exhalation and the lowering of the body through compression. Your hand should not revolve around the spinal column. It should revolve because your entire body is turning.

The physical advantage of this kata is that the perception center of the hand becomes more open, the upper half of the body is free, and the feet become increasingly rooted. The lowering of the elbows combined with the stretching of the wrists encourages the thoracic cage to expand, the shoulders to relax, and tension and suspended emotion to drop, and produces relaxed breathing. By the same token it prevents your body from moving like a bouncing ball.

The hand accompanies the compression and helps regulate the pressure put on the snow. Throughout the turn, the hand remains in the same vertical axis parallel to the spinal column, which enables the skwaller to maintain the body in alignment with the feet.

Kata 8: Compression/Extension on a Steep Slope

When gliding down a steep slope, or in powder, or over bumps, you will flex your legs in order to maintain contact as you go through the fall line, then extend the legs to maintain contact and complete the turn.

The warm-up exercise is done on a flat surface and consists of visualizing skiing a curve in a compressed stance. You push off on the front foot to enter the turn, then extending upward and behind the middle of the foot for the phase of coming out of the turn.

This kata can be used on a gentle slope in order to make wide traverses. While this exercise is pleasant to do because of the sensations it provides, it is not considered a high-performance movement for competition.

CHAPTER 10

The Art of Gliding, the Art of Living

It has been my misfortune to observe in the sports world countless people who, not being able to reach the highest level of their sport for a variety of reasons—an accident, health issues, insufficient training, lack of self-confidence—find themselves frustrated, depressed, and aimless. Getting people back on track is difficult when they believe they have already failed their dream, although it is still possible for them to carry on and achieve some worthy results. The systems for high-level athletes are not equipped to follow these individuals psychologically to the end of their journey. For this reason, these individuals remain consumed by regret or bitterness about feeling incomplete, some for their entire lives.

In the training of these competitors, nothing prepares them for the worst, for the ultimate setback. Trainers have an important responsibility, as they all know that many are called but few are chosen. In their building of athletes from the most tender age, trainers should give meaning to the activity. Of course, the primary objective is to achieve results, but this is not all. High-level sports training should also provide support for personal development and preparation for an active life, especially for the athlete who will be leaving by the back door. It is not merely

a question of professional retraining, but a discovery of one's other potentials.

Ski instruction should also provide a meaning for each movement. The study of the mental, emotional, and physical self gives the skier access to a unit of three poles within—mind, heart, body. Deeply planted in her feet, centered within her belly during the action, her mind and emotions calm, the skier is able to confront the most difficult situations. This apprenticeship should be the central concern of a skier's instructors throughout the duration of her training. When the day arrives that the competitor needs to find some new activity on which to focus her efforts, all the resources she requires will be found within. The force is with her.

A loss of motivation is often observed in the young during adolescence. Excessive training, constant judgments on the part of the coach or teacher, the repetition and correction of a movement a thousand times, relational problems inside the group, and other interests can all be sources of this loss of motivation.

What can we do to keep the flame that animates a young athlete alive?

When the young competitor continues to win over the years, everything is fine. Then one day he becomes disenchanted because results require patience, and he does not want to wait. Bigger tests are introduced, the opponents are stronger, an injury persists, or he begins to simply doubt his abilities or desire to continue. The coach preaches and tries to motivate him—and nothing comes of it.

So what would the best recipe be in such a situation? In training, the instructors too often forget the psychological and emotional aspect of the athlete, because they never received any training themselves in this regard. They try to muddle through these rough patches with calls for teamwork and confidence. But the young athlete can still perceive the fragility inside that is the source of his discomfort, and he has the impression that he is the only one to feel this way. Study of human behavior and consequently of oneself is therefore a significant antidote. The best approach is to not wait for the crisis to appear. The training period should be done step by step, in tandem with and during the acquisition of sport technique.

. . .

Over the course of this book we have learned how to take into consideration both our body and our environment for the purpose of skiing (or snowboarding or skwalling) better. Little by little the battle against the forces (those we think are external) that prevent us from realizing what we want transforms into a relationship that leans toward the harmonizing of the forces that are present. We make a transition from a dualistic relationship to a united relationship.

Snow sports can teach us this, *if* we manage to get ourselves attuned. From the simple physical phenomenon that provides sensations and emotions, we have the possibility of opening a space of new perceptions within ourselves. Once the breech has been opened, the direction is provided. Body and mind become as one, emptying themselves of fears and certitudes, and the tensions accompanying them. The skier becomes aware that she belongs to this world and is not separate from it, as the all-powerful mind too often tries to make her believe. But old habits always lie in wait, and will take possession of anyone who relaxes his or her vigilance.

This sport of gliding becomes an art when the skier (or snowboarder or skwaller) realizes that there is a connection, a parallel between his life as a skier in nature and his everyday life as a human being in the world.

The glider should initially discover, use, and master the three poles that are within:

- The mind: The seat of thought and decision, the mind is primarily a tool, a control tower, a center for processing information.
- The heart: The seat of emotion and love, the connection between the head and the body, the linking point between the interior and the exterior (through the breath), the heart joins and harmonizes the different poles of the body where their paths cross.
- The body: The seat of locomotion, through study and training the body moves from the status of a physical entity that holds one back to that of the attuned body.

Over the course of this work, the skier gradually discovers that he is not his thoughts, his emotions, or all or part of his body, but he is the awareness that he is existing. The art of gliding truly becomes an art of living when we become capable of applying the three pillars of the art of gliding to daily life. Those pillars are:

- Being attuned to and respecting the body, which helps in maintaining good health and a good connection to one's environment
- Being attuned to and respecting one's environment, both human society and the natural world
- Applying the laws that govern movement and protecting the body and the environment.

The bottom line: Respect, listen, and act, but also protect and preserve what should be and take part in the evolution of the whole through our actions.

We have an influence on everything that surrounds us simply by our presence, by our way of handling situations, family and social problems, and the natural environment. The way we feed ourselves, take care of ourselves, and how and what we consume all have implications for our body and for nature.

Man has long believed that he can force nature to bend to his will. Today studies show that our ancestral societies were able to find a balance between man and nature, whereas modern society leads to excess consumption, pollution, and the separation of man and nature (for example, the creation of megalopolises and the accelerated exodus from rural regions).

The problems facing us are numerous and immense. We have a tendency to think that we are not able to do anything by ourselves in our own little corners, but we should never forget that there are no small actions.

Listening, seeing, understanding, feeling: all go into the preparation of right action. This is true in any context: competitions, love life, family life, social life. For the action to be right, it is necessary to integrate all the data specific to a given situation. When we ski, the surrounding environment is practically stable and allows us to discover our ambiguities as well as our fluidity in a specific defined activity. In society, the environment is changing ceaselessly and there are countless parameters. Adapting is much more complex.

Despite everything, nature remains a formidable field of experimentation of life. When, by performing an activity in nature, the skier discovers centered action, his entire life will be changed. The centered action goes beyond the athletic context and intervenes in everything that goes into making up a life. Centered action is the exact opposite of an ego-motivated action. It involves a strong point within that is the source of right action.

If in the beginning skiing is a leisure activity based on a search for pleasure, it becomes, thanks to the interior development it can trigger, an opening to oneself and to the world. The quest for having and the desire to consume space and sensations are transformed into self-realization that is in tune with one's surroundings.

The skier who no longer identifies with his mind, his emotions, his body will discover a spiritual dimension within. The mists created by the mind will dissipate. The mind will become clear and fast as lightning. The emotions that have been soothed will give way to a feeling of oneness, of love for everything that goes into making a life. The body that is now relaxed and free of the stranglehold of the tyrannical mind becomes fluid, aware, and light with centered movement and conscious action.

For the novice, the leisure activity of skiing (or snowboarding or skwalling) will become, with practice, a lifestyle with its own clothing codes, jargon, attitudes. The group, the tribe, gives the illusion of belonging to a caste of initiates.

The art of gliding is born at a point beyond this social behavior. The art of gliding is a practice that shuns appearances and is a way of being true. It births athletes who are artists of the turn, respectful of the environment and aware of their place in the world. The art of living follows from this attitude. The practitioner becomes more spiritual, and ceaselessly recenters his energy to better position himself and act in his body, society, and nature. The art of living is this ability to make our body and our mind the channel of that fundamental energy within each of us, the essence of our essence that is forever seeking expression.

Physical activities are good schools for discovering our behavior patterns, our blockages, and finally, our true selves.

The art of gliding leads to the art of living. A glider's approach speaks volumes about his personality and provides proof that everything is connected. A physical action that is truly conscious and centered will, little by little, lead the glider to perform conscious acts in everyday life, including in his life choices, the positions he takes, and the actions he makes.

Man is constantly in quest of somewhere else to be and some other way to be. Carried away by his enthusiasm, his imagination works on ways to colonize Mars but forgets that he is in the process of destroying the Earth, which is by far more interesting and alive than the red planet. Overly extended toward an elsewhere, he loses his roots. The energy deployed in the conquest of space could be better used for other purposes (the quality of life on Earth, for example).

When gliding, one has the opportunity to directly measure the short-term effects of forgetting one's roots. Becoming uprooted inevitably leads to a fall. Staying grounded in society requires taking care of and protecting our planet, supporting the survival of the human race, mutual aid and solidarity among people, political stability, and peace. Without any of this, what is the use of searching elsewhere, except for someplace to run away to?

Conclusion

In our culture, we have a tendency to give preference and credit to the hard-working types who do not discuss things, and who apply and follow to the letter the instructions set by their fathers, without flinching or complaining. Do you believe that, in this state of mind, the magic living inside each one of us can find the means to express itself? For a world to evolve and change, it must offer flexible structures and accept differences.

The duty of the coach is above all to accompany his students like a responsible father, all throughout their itinerary, by helping them to discover themselves, get past their blockages, and by preparing them to face difficult situations. Skiing is a beautiful school of life. One can find in gliding all states of being and all kinds of situations.

This book has been focused on the question of technique, but not on the level of a specific move to acquire. It involves the great physical laws, applied to the body, which one should know in order to be able to express oneself in this domain without having to forget one's own sensibilities. This work on the body is more a labor of harmonization than it is a technique. It offers another way to communicate with oneself. But the person who throws himself into this journey of self-discovery needs to realize that a certain time will be required to empty himself of his former certitudes in order to have room for new ones. When the skier is in between the two, a void appears, and she can have the impression at that moment that she is regressing or going astray. This temporary regression is necessary. It is the doorway into the new, which still exists in the state of potential.

I have been trying with this essay to share my journey in the world of gliding over snow with you. The desire to refine my perceptions and understand phenomena has been my main motivation. This desire, this tension directed toward an elsewhere, to my astonishment brought me back to myself and enabled me to look at my environment in another way. I hope that these pages will have let you feel what, for me, represents much more than sports activity—an art of gliding that gradually leads us to an art of living beyond styles and tendencies, permeating our certitudes and gestures day after day.

...

Life is a great inner glide
So let's keep gliding!
With exquisite pleasure . . .
Until later my friend!

Bibliography

These are the authors who helped me discover the potentials of my body, my heart, and my mind.

English Titles

Capra, Fritjof. *The Tao of Physics*. Boston: Shambhala, 2000.

Herrigel, Eugen. *Zen in the Art of Archery*. New York: Vintage, 1999.

French Titles

de Alcantara, Pedro. *La technique Alexander*. Paris: Editions Dangles, 1997.

Cauhépé, J.-D., and A. Kuang. *Hara architecture du milieu juste*. Paris: Guy Trédaniel, 1987.

Coquet, Michel. *Budo ésoterique ou la voie des arts martiaux*. Paris: Editions l'Or du Temps, 1991.

———. *Iaido or l'art de trancher l'ego*. Paris: Editions l'Or du Temps, 1991.

de Coulon, Jacques. *Paix et yoga*. Paris: Editions Chiron, 1985.

Desjardins, Arnaud. *À la recherché du soi 1, 2, 3,* and *4*. Paris: Editions la Table Ronde, 1979.

Dioptaz, Michel-Laurent. *Sarbacana*. Paris: Editions le Souffle d'Or, 1993.

Liu, Da. *Taï Chi Chuan et Yi King*. Paris: Editions Chiron Sports, 1986.

Lowen, Alexander. *La bio-énergie*. Paris: Editions Robert Lafond, 1995.

Manent, Geneviève. *La relaxation au quotidian*. Paris: Editions le Souffle d'Or, 2001.

Masterton, Ailsa. *La technique Alexander*. Paris: Editions Könemann, 1999.

Naslednikov, Mitsou (Ma Anand Margo). *Tantra Le chemin de l'extase*. Paris: Albin Michel, 1981.

Sionnet, Christine. *L'art de la vague et le sabre*. Paris: Editions le Souffle d'Or, 1998.

Index

Books of Related Interest

The Five Tibetans
Five Dynamic Exercises for Health, Energy, and Personal Power
by Christopher S. Kilham

The Yin Yoga Kit
The Practice of Quiet Power
by Biff Mithoefer

Pilates on the Ball
The World's Most Popular Workout Using the Exercise Ball
by Colleen Craig

Martial Arts Teaching Tales of Power and Paradox
Freeing the Mind, Focusing Chi, and Mastering the Self
by Pascal Fauliot

Energy Balance through the Tao
Exercises for Cultivating Yin Energy
by Mantak Chia

The Secret Teachings of the Tao Te Ching
by Mantak Chia and Tao Huang

The Tao of Voice
A New East-West Approach to Transforming
the Singing and Speaking Voice
by Stephen Chun-Tao Cheng

The Spiritual Foundations of Aikido
by William Gleason

Inner Traditions • Bear & Company
P.O. Box 388
Rochester, VT 05767
1-800-246-8648
www.InnerTraditions.com

Or contact your local bookseller